Real Time Analytics with SAP HANA

Enhance your SAP HANA skills using this step-by-step guide to create data models and reports for real time analytics

Vinay Singh

BIRMINGHAM - MUMBAI

Real Time Analytics with SAP HANA

First published: October 2015

Production reference: 1261015

Published by Packt Publishing Ltd.
Livery Place
35 Livery Street
Birmingham B3 2PB, UK.

ISBN 978-1-78217-411-0

www.packtpub.com

Credits

Author
Vinay Singh

Reviewers
Yatindra Mehta
Joselyn Quintero Veliz

Commissioning Editor
Kunal Parikh

Acquisition Editor
Reshma Raman

Content Development Editor
Anand Singh

Technical Editor
Utkarsha S. Kadam

Copy Editors
Kausambhi Majumdar
Merilyn Pereira
Alpha Singh

Project Coordinator
Paushali Desai

Proofreader
Safis Editing

Indexer
Rekha Nair

Graphics
Jason Monteiro

Production Coordinator
Melwyn Dsa

Cover Work
Melwyn Dsa

About the Author

Vinay Singh has MBA and BE (CS) degrees and is a SAP HANA/BI architect at Freudenberg Sealing Technology, Germany, working in the SAP Analytics area. He has nearly 10 years of SAP experience in the field of SAP product development and consulting. Before joining Freudenberg, he worked with companies such as SAP Labs, Adobe, and T-systems, which gave him a good mix of product development and consulting experience.

He has been an author and coauthor on numerous articles in various journals and has officially reviewed a couple of books on SAP Analytics topics. He is also a visiting faculty at Hochschule Furtwangen University, BW, where he teaches SAP HANA under the SAP UCC program.

It is a pleasure to acknowledge the help that I had with the preparation of this text.

The first mention goes to my wife, Minal, for her understating of the time I was spending on the book and her time-to-time feedback.

Many individuals have provided comments at various stages on portions of this book. Thanks to my parents, Naveen Rai, Soraya Dastager, Taha Mahmoud, and Shehab Hindam for their continuous support and encouragement and Bhavesh Ratnam, George Varghese, Munmun Singhania, and Kamalbasha Shafi for their direct / indirect contribution to the various chapters of the book. Special thanks to Joselyn Quintero and Yatindra Mehta for finding time to review the book and help make it better. I would like to appreciate and thank my publishing team and graphics team for their splendid work.

Finally, I sincerely thank my editors who worked closely with me: Anand Singh, Utkarsha S. Kadam, and Reshma Raman, without whom the book would not have been possible.

About the Reviewers

Yatindra Mehta is a SAP HANA architect and expert employed with SAP labs. He has been working in the SAP domain for around 10 years. He has executed various projects for manufacturing, retail, automotive, and telecommunications customers. He has served various prestigious customers in his career such as Siemens(SHC), T-COM, and Toyota to name a few. Currenlty, he works on the SAP HANA technology and helps customer leverage the SAP HANA technology, SLT, and so on.

I would like to thank Vinay, who gave me this opportunity to review his book. This is a really wondeful book, written precisely for learners in a simple and arcticulated way. Also, I would like to thank the publishers for publishing this amazing book.

Joselyn Quintero Veliz is a Venezuelan financial expert and SAP Financials senior consultant, with professional experience in the technology, oil, construction, manufacturing, and banking industries. Managing both business and technology environments, she is able to transform financial requirements into successful IT solutions. She possesses a certification of In-Memory Technology Databases for SAP HANA, issued by the Hasso Plattner Institute in Postdam, Germany.

Currently, Joselyn works as a freelance SAP process excellence senior consultant, helping companies take advantage of the latest SAP technologies to reach ambitious business goals.

In her free time, Joselyn spreads her personal financial knowledge across Latin America, through her website `http://www.joselynquintero.com/`. Joselyn also works in philanthropic initiatives as a Spanish translator at Animal Foundation Platform, promoting the ethical treatment of, and reducing the violence against, stray animals.

I want to first thank the author of the book for sharing valuable knowledge in these pages, providing useful information for people around the world. Secondly, I'd like to thank Packt Publishing for promoting high-level knowledge, and for inviting me to be part of this project. Last, but not least, I appreciate my family and friends for their support and patience and for not being there during the hours this book required my focus. We worked as a team, and we got it!

www.PacktPub.com

Support files, eBooks, discount offers, and more

For support files and downloads related to your book, please visit www.PacktPub.com.

Did you know that Packt offers eBook versions of every book published, with PDF and ePub files available? You can upgrade to the eBook version at www.PacktPub.com and as a print book customer, you are entitled to a discount on the eBook copy. Get in touch with us at service@packtpub.com for more details.

At www.PacktPub.com, you can also read a collection of free technical articles, sign up for a range of free newsletters and receive exclusive discounts and offers on Packt books and eBooks.

https://www2.packtpub.com/books/subscription/packtlib

Do you need instant solutions to your IT questions? PacktLib is Packt's online digital book library. Here, you can search, access, and read Packt's entire library of books.

Why subscribe?

- Fully searchable across every book published by Packt
- Copy and paste, print, and bookmark content
- On demand and accessible via a web browser

Free access for Packt account holders

If you have an account with Packt at www.PacktPub.com, you can use this to access PacktLib today and view 9 entirely free books. Simply use your login credentials for immediate access.

Instant updates on new Packt books

Get notified! Find out when new books are published by following @PacktEnterprise on Twitter or the *Packt Enterprise* Facebook page.

Table of Contents

Preface

Real-time analytics is revolutionizing the way we interact with customers, partners and system in totality. The continuous evolution of technology is changing the way we do business. Uncertainty and change in the global marketplace is driving new ideas and innovation. Competing in this new hyper-connected and digitized world requires a new business platform that meets the demand for speed and innovation with reduced complexity. The demand for real-time data and analytics is so pervasive that every customer, big or small, wants to have it.

Real-time analytics is basically the use of (or to have an option to use) all the available data and resources within the enterprise as and when they are needed. The term real-time analytics implies practically instant access and use of analytical data.

As it turns out, to answer this need and the changes in the business, SAP came up with a complete out-of-the-box solution, transforming the database industry by combining database, data processing, and application platform capabilities into a single in-memory platform called SAP HANA. SAP HANA makes it possible for applications and analytics to run without information processing latency. It also allows to build sense and response solutions on a large volume of real-time data without thinking of pre-aggregates.

To answer why you should choose SAP HANA for real-time analytics, we would have a look at the key capabilities of SAP HANA, such as Massive speed—the scan speed of the SAP HANA database is 3.19 billion symbol per second per core (in lab conditions). High efficiencies—if you port the data from a classical database to SAP HANA, eliminating unnecessary indexes and aggregate tables and allowing operational reporting directly on SAP HANA, the data footprint could be reduced by a factor of as high as 37. The data compression rate is approximately 4 to 1. Lower cost providing a dual OLTP—the OLAP architecture reduces the data footprint, which saves on storage costs.

Eliminating the need for data extraction and transfer from OLAP to OLTP saves time and resources. Flexibility—SAP HANA is an ideal big data analytics platform, capable of efficiently loading and rapidly analyzing multiple data types in both structured and unstructured forms.

While there are many tools in the market for real-time analytics, this book discusses how we can use all the preceding mentioned features of SAP HANA and design our data models for real-time analytics. We will be working on SAP HANA as a sidecar / standalone scenario to create our data models. This book is organized into four parts, discussing various concepts related to data modeling.

This book has a particular structure, as follows:

- Setting up the platform:

  Chapters 1, 2, and 3, describe how we can setup the platform for SAP HANA

- Creating data models:

  Chapters 4 and 5 explain how to create data models in SAP HANA

- Supporting concepts of data modeling:

  Chapters 6 and 7 elaborate the supporting concepts to create data models in SAP HANA

- Reporting on data models:

  Chapters 8 and 9 deal with the creation of reports

What this book covers

Chapter 1, Kickoff – Before We Start, sets the basic concepts and building blocks for the book. It talks about the prerequisite development skill that you must have before we plunge into data modeling.

Chapter 2, SAP HANA Data Modeling Approach, covers the approach to SAP HANA data modeling and the do's and dont's while creating data models.

Chapter 3, Different Ways of SAP HANA Data Load, teaches you how to load data into SAP HANA, explore various options of data load as per the data source and need, understand real-time replication via SLT, and use SAP HANA Studio for the Data Load.

Chapter 4, Creating SAP HANA Artifacts Attribute Views and Analytical Views, teaches you how to create HANA artifacts—Attribute view and Analytical view. You will learn the various other components involved during the creation of these Artifacts.

Chapter 5, Creating SAP HANA Artifacts – Analytical Privileges and Calculation Views, teaches you how to create HANA artifacts—Analytical privileges and Calculation views. You will learn the various other components involved in the creation of these Artifacts.

Chapter 6, Understanding Text Search and Hierarchies in SAP HANA, talks about hierarchies and Text Search in SAP HANA, how to create and use them in our data models for real time analytics, how to create and use Full Text Search, how to create hierarchies as per usage, and understanding the concept of parent-child hierarchies and level hierarchies.

Chapter 7, Using Decision Tables and Transporting SAP HANA Content, teaches you how to work with additional capabilities of SAP HANA such as decision tables and currency conversion. You will also learn how our SAP HANA Artifacts can be transported across the landscape.

Chapter 8, Consuming SAP HANA Data Models, teaches you reporting with SAP HANA data models by using your own data models created in previous chapters for reporting. It also talks of a general overview of all the tools available in SAP HANA.

Chapter 9, An Introduction to Application Function Library, explores the AFL library. You will learn how the deliver prepackaged functionality can be used in building information models faster and in an easier way. It will also discuss the AFL deliver prepackaged functionality, which will help us to know what the inbuilt functions are that can be used without reworking/redeveloping.

What you need for this book

We will consider only the software requirement for the end user perspective. You will need to have SAP HANA Studio installed on your client machines and should have access to the SAP HANA server instance. We discuss the steps to add an instance to SAP HANA Studio in *Chapter 2, SAP HANA Data Modeling Approach.*

The software requirements are as follows:

- Sap HANA Studio 1.0 REV 80 or later (mandatory)
- SAP HANA database clients 1.0 REV80 (mandatory)
- SAP Design Studio on 1.5 (optional)
- SAP Data Services 4.2 SP1 (optional)
- SAP Business Intelligence Platform 4.1 SP2 (optional)

Who this book is for

If you are a SAP HANA data modeler, developer, implementation/migration consultant, project manager, or architect who is responsible for implementing/migrating to SAP HANA, this book is for you.

Conventions

In this book, you will find a number of text styles that distinguish between different kinds of information. Here are some examples of these styles and an explanation of their meaning.

Code words in text, database table names, folder names, filenames, file extensions, pathnames, dummy URLs, user input, and Twitter handles are shown as follows: "We can include other contexts through the use of the `include` directive."

A block of code is set as follows:

```
CREATE PROCEDURE {schema.}name
            {({IN|OUT|INOUT}
                      param_name data_type {,...})}
            {LANGUAGE <LANG>} {SQL SECURITY <MODE>}
            {READS SQL DATA {WITH RESULT VIEW <view_name>}} AS
BEGIN
  ...
END
```

Any command-line input or output is written as follows:

```
GRANT SELECT ON SCHEMA <YOUR SCHEMA> TO _SYS_REPO WITH GRANT OPTION;
GRANT SELECT ON SCHEMA HANA_DEMO TO _SYS_REPO WITH GRANT OPTION
```

New terms and **important words** are shown in bold. Words that you see on the screen, for example, in menus or dialog boxes, appear in the text like this: "You can see the created procedure below our schema under the **Procedures...** folder."

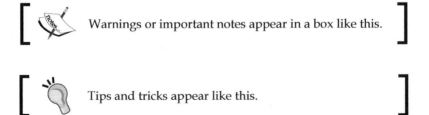

Warnings or important notes appear in a box like this.

Tips and tricks appear like this.

Reader feedback

Feedback from our readers is always welcome. Let us know what you think about this book—what you liked or disliked. Reader feedback is important for us as it helps us develop titles that you will really get the most out of.

To send us general feedback, simply e-mail feedback@packtpub.com, and mention the book's title in the subject of your message.

If there is a topic that you have expertise in and you are interested in either writing or contributing to a book, see our author guide at www.packtpub.com/authors.

Customer support

Now that you are the proud owner of a Packt book, we have a number of things to help you to get the most from your purchase.

Downloading the example code

You can download the example code files from your account at http://www.packtpub.com for all the Packt Publishing books you have purchased. If you purchased this book elsewhere, you can visit http://www.packtpub.com/support and register to have the files e-mailed directly to you.

Downloading the color images of this book

We also provide you with a PDF file that has color images of the screenshots/diagrams used in this book. The color images will help you better understand the changes in the output. You can download this file from https://www.packtpub.com/sites/default/files/downloads/4110EN.pdf.

Errata

Although we have taken every care to ensure the accuracy of our content, mistakes do happen. If you find a mistake in one of our books—maybe a mistake in the text or the code—we would be grateful if you could report this to us. By doing so, you can save other readers from frustration and help us improve subsequent versions of this book. If you find any errata, please report them by visiting http://www.packtpub.com/submit-errata, selecting your book, clicking on the **Errata Submission Form** link, and entering the details of your errata. Once your errata are verified, your submission will be accepted and the errata will be uploaded to our website or added to any list of existing errata under the Errata section of that title.

To view the previously submitted errata, go to https://www.packtpub.com/books/ content/support and enter the name of the book in the search field. The required information will appear under the **Errata** section.

Piracy

Piracy of copyrighted material on the Internet is an ongoing problem across all media. At Packt, we take the protection of our copyright and licenses very seriously. If you come across any illegal copies of our works in any form on the Internet, please provide us with the location address or website name immediately so that we can pursue a remedy.

Please contact us at copyright@packtpub.com with a link to the suspected pirated material.

We appreciate your help in protecting our authors and our ability to bring you valuable content.

Questions

If you have a problem with any aspect of this book, you can contact us at questions@packtpub.com, and we will do our best to address the problem.

1
Kickoff – Before We Start

This chapter intends to provide context and background to set the base with which we can manipulate the datasets to be used for data modeling. This section tries to act as a refresher that should help you understand and pick up modeling topics faster in upcoming chapters.

We start the chapter with **Structured Query Language (SQL)** – how we can use it for controlling and manipulating the SAP HANA database objects and data. Then we move on to create SQLscript and learn how to use it effectively. We will also discuss creation and call of procedure step by step in this chapter, which is a good tool for the upcoming topics. We will end the chapter with a detailed discussion on JOINS and how it can be used for connecting tables in SAP HANA.

After completing this chapter you will be able to:

- Understand and use SAP HANA SQL statements
- Create SQLscript and use it
- Create and call a procedure
- Connect tables using SAP HANA specific JOINS

Introducing SAP HANA SQL

As stated, you will not learn SQL as a whole new concept, but will just revise the traditional SQL concepts at a glance and focus on a few new topics that are of importance from SAP HANA perspective. Our key focus here will be on the SAP HANA SQL script, creating procedures, and learning to create SAP HANA specific JOINS.

Classical SQL

SQL is used to retrieve, store, and manipulate data in the database. SQL can be studied under three subheads:

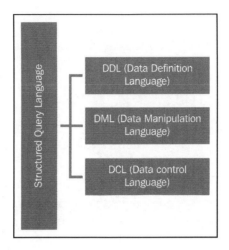

These subheads are explained as follows:

- **DDL**: These statement that are used to define the data: `create`, `alter`, `drop` **tables**
- **DML**: These statements are used to manipulate the data, `select`, `deselect`, `insert`, and `update`
- **DCL**: These statements that are used to control the `table`, `grant`, and revoke

The followings are the elements of SQL:

- **Identifiers**: These are used to represent names in SQL statements including table/view name, column name, username, role name and so on. There are two types of Identifiers: ordinary and delimited.
- **Data types**: These define the characteristics of the data and its value. Data types in SQL are as follows:

Categories	Data type
Numeric	`float`, `real`, `integer`, `decimal`, `double`, `tinyint`, `small int`, and `small decimal`
Large	`blob`, `clob`, `nclob`, and `text`

Categories	Data type
Binary	varbinary
Character string	varchar, nvarchar, alphanum, and shorttext.
Date	time, date, secondtime, and timestamp

- **Expressions**: These are clause evaluated to return values. We have different types of expressions in SQL. For example, if...then.....else (case expression) or nested queries (Select (Select ......)).

- **Functions**: These are used in expressions for retrieving information from the database. We have a number of functions and data type conversion functions. The number functions take numeric values or alphanumeric/strings with numeric character values and return numeric values, whereas, data type conversion functions are used to convert arguments from one data type to another. For example, to_alphanum, concat, current_date, and so on.

- **Operators**: These are used for value comparison, assigning values, or can also be used for calculation. We have different types of operators like Unary, Binary, arithmetic, and string operators to name a few. For example, +, =, subtraction, and or.

- **Predicates**: A predicate is specified by combining one or more expressions or logical operators and returning one of the following logical or truth values: true, false, or unknown. Examples are null, in, and like.

In the upcoming chapters, we will learn how to work with SAP HANA studio and open SQL editor, so as to complete the concepts. I will show you how we work with the preceding SQL concepts. For our examples and exercises, we will use the following tables. We will create more tables in further chapters as we progress.

The following table shows you the sales_facts:

PRODUCT_ KEY	REGION_ KEY	AMOUNT_ SOLD	QUANTITY_ SOLD
01	100	50000	500
02	200	60000	600
03	300	20000	200

The following table shows you the CUSTOMERS data:

CUSTOMER_KEY	CUST_LAST_NAME	CUST_FIRST_NAME
C1	Mehta	Yatin
C2	Aguirre	Tomas
C3	Huber	Ralf

The following is a REGION table:

REGION_ID	REGION_NAME	SUB_AREA
100	Europe	Germany
200	Asia	Japan
300	US	Northfields

The following table shows you details of the PRODUCT table:

PRODUCT_KEY	PRODUCT_NAME
01	GasKit
02	RubberWasher

Let's see how we can create the preceding tables in SAP HANA:

1. In SAP HANA studio, right-clicking on your schema (here, **HANA_DEMO**) will display **Open SQL Console**; click on it.

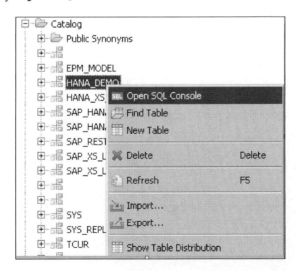

2. We will cover some of the following SQL queries to create the tables:

Create a schema first, if it hasn't already been created for you— HANA_DEMO; you can choose any name.

A database schema is the skeleton structure that represents the logical view of the entire database (objects such as tables, views, and stored procedures). It defines how the data is organized and how the relations among them are associated. It formulates all the constraints that are to be applied on the data, whereas Table is one of the objects contained in schema. It is a set of data elements (values) that is organized using a model of vertical columns (which are identified by their name) and horizontal rows:

```
CREATE SCHEMA "HANA_DEMO";
```

```
GRANT SELECT ON SCHEMA HANA_DEMO TO _SYS_REPO WITH GRANT OPTION;
if you do not run Grant , later when you will activate your views
it will give you erros.
```

The following command creates the SALES_FACTS table:

```
CREATE   COLUMN TABLE "HANA_DEMO"."SALES_FACTS"(

"PRODUCT_KEY" INTEGER NOT NULL,

"REGION_KEY" INTEGER NOT NULL,

"AMOUNT_SOLD" DECIMAL NOT NULL,

"QUANTITY_SOLD" INTEGER NOT NULL,

PRIMARY KEY ("PRODUCT_KEY","REGION_KEY") );
```

The following command creates the CUSTOMER table:

```
CREATE   COLUMN TABLE "HANA_DEMO"."CUSTOMER"(

"CUSTOMER_KEY" VARCHAR(8) NOT NULL,

"CUST_LAST_NAME" VARCHAR(100) NULL,

"CUST_FIRST_NAME" VARCHAR(30) NULL,

PRIMARY KEY ("CUSTOMER_KEY ") );
```

The following command creates the PRODUCTS table:

```
CREATE   COLUMN TABLE "HANA_DEMO"."PRODUCTS" (

"PRODUCT_KEY" INTEGER NOT NULL,

"PRODUCT_NAME" VARCHAR(50) NULL,

PRIMARY KEY ("PRODUCT_KEY") );
```

The following command creates the REGION table:

```
CREATE   COLUMN TABLE "HANA_DEMO"."REGION"(

"REGION_ID" INTEGER NOT NULL,

"REGION_NAME" VARCHAR(100) NULL,
```

```
"SUB_AREA" VARCHAR(30) NULL,
PRIMARY KEY ("REGION_ID") );
```

The following are sample `insert` queries:

```
insert into "<YOUR SCHEMA>"."TABLE NAME"
values(columns1,Columns2,..,);
insert into "HANA_DEMO"."SALES_FACTS" values(01,100,50000,500);
insert into "HANA_DEMO"."PRODUCTS" values(01,'GasKit');
insert into "HANA_DEMO"."REGION" values(01,'Europe','Germany');
```

 I am inserting single values, but you can insert or re-run the query with different values or download the Excel file from our website for demo data.

3. After executing the scripts, you should have three tables created. If there are no tables, try right-clicking on your schema and then refresh it.

    In the following screenshot, you can see the tables we just created under the **HANA_DEMO** schema:

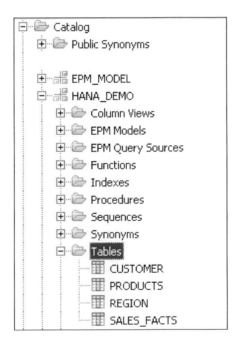

[We need to Grant schema SELECT rights to _SYS_REPO user.]

In SQL, the editor of our schema needs to execute the following command line:

```
GRANT SELECT ON SCHEMA <YOUR SCHEMA> TO _SYS_REPO WITH GRANT OPTION;
GRANT SELECT ON SCHEMA HANA_DEMO TO _SYS_REPO WITH GRANT OPTION
```

If we miss this step, an error will occur when you activate your views later.

The SAP HANA SQLscript

In the following section, we will learn about the SAP HANA SQLscript and see the additional capabilities it brings along with it.

Why SQLscript?

SQLscript is a collection of extensions in **Structured Query Language (SQL)**. The main motivation for SQLscript is to push data intensive application logic into the database, which was not being done in the classical approach where the application logic is mostly executed in an application layer.

We have the following extensions for SQLscript:

Extension	Usage
Datatype extension (create/drop type)	This allows definition of table type without corresponding tables
Procedural extension (create procedure)	This is an imperative construct to push data intensive logic into the database
Functional extension (create function)	This creates side-effect free scalar or table functions, which can be used to express and encapsulate complex data flows

How different is an SQLscript in SAP HANA from classical SQL queries?

Let's do a comparative study between an SQLscript in SAP HANA and classical SQL queries to find out what the point of differences are, as shown in the following table:

SQLscript in SAP HANA	Classical SQL
Multiple result sets can be returned	Query returns only single result set
More database intensive, codes are executed at DB layer, gives better performance	Limited executions at DB layer resulting in multiple access to and from database, relatively slow performance
Control logics such as if/else and business logics like currency conversion can be easily expressed	SQL queries do not have such features
Gives more flexibility to developer to use imperative and declarative logics together	No such flexibility with SQL queries
Supports local variables for intermediate result sets with implicit types	Globally visible views need to be defined even for intermediate result sets or steps
Parameterization of views is possible	Parameterization of views is not possible

The following figure shows you a graphical comparison of the classical approach and the SAP HANA approach:

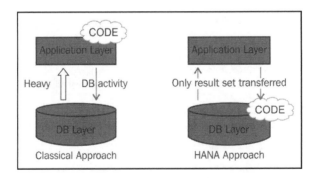

When should we use SQLscript?

SQLscript should be used in cases where other modeling constructs of SAP HANA, for example, analytic views or attribute views are not sufficient.

Procedures

Procedures are reusable processing blocks that are implemented using the SQLscript, which describes a sequence of operations on data passed as input and database tables. It can be created as read-only (without side-effects) or read-write (with side-effects).

Procedures can have multiple input parameters and output parameters (can be scalar or table types).

There are three different ways to create a procedure in HANA:

- Using the SQL editor (in SAP HANA Studio)
- Using the **Modeler** wizard in the modeler perspective (in SAP HANA Studio)
- Using the SAP HANA XS project in the **SAP HANA Development** perspective (in SAP HANA Studio), which isn't discussed in this chapter

Creating with the SQL editor (in SAP HANA Studio)

The following syntax is used to create procedure via the SQL editor:

```
CREATE PROCEDURE {schema.}name
        {({IN|OUT|INOUT}
                    param_name data_type {,...})}
        {LANGUAGE <LANG>} {SQL SECURITY <MODE>}
        {READS SQL DATA {WITH RESULT VIEW <view_name>}} AS
BEGIN
...
END
```

> **Downloading the example code**
>
> You can download the example code files from your account at `http://www.packtpub.com` for all the Packt Publishing books you have purchased. If you purchased this book elsewhere, you can visit `http://www.packtpub.com/support` and register to have the files e-mailed directly to you.

The parameters are for:

- **Reads SQL Data**: This defines a procedure as read-only.
- **Language**: This specifies the implementation. SQLscript is the default language.
- **With result view**: This is used to create a column view for the output parameter of the type table.

Let's create a procedure where we will pass discount as the input parameter and get the sales report as the output parameter. We use the same tables that we created previously:

```
CREATE PROCEDURE HANA_DEMO."PROC_EU_SALES_REPORT"(
          IN DISCOUNT INTEGER,
          OUT OUTPUT_TABLE HANA_DEMO."EU_SALES" )
LANGUAGE SQLSCRIPT SQL SECURITY INVOKER AS
/*********BEGIN PROCEDURE SCRIPT ************/
BEGIN
Pvar1 = SELECT T1.REGION_NAME, T1.SUB_AREA, T2.PRODUCT_KEY, T2.AMOUNT_
SOLD
          FROM HANA_DEMO.REGION AS T1
          INNER JOIN
          HANA_DEMO.SALES_FACT AS T2
          ON T1.REGION_KEY = T2.REGION_KEY;

Pvar2 = SELECT T1.REGION_NAME, T1.SUB_AREA, T1.PRODUCT_KEY, T1.AMOUNT_
SOLD, T2.PRODUCT_NAME
          FROM :Pvar1 AS T1
          INNER JOIN
          HANA_DEMO.PRODUCT AS T2
          ON T1.PRODUCT_KEY = T2.PRODUCT_KEY;

OUTPUT_TABLE = SELECT SUM(AMOUNT_SOLD) AS AMOUNT_SOLD, SUM(AMOUNT_SOLD
- (AMOUNT_SOLD * :DISCOUNT/ 100)) AS NET_AMOUNT,
          PRODUCT_NAME, REGION_NAME, SUB_AREA
          FROM :Pvar2
          GROUP BY PRODUCT_NAME, REGION_NAME, SUB_AREA;
END;
```

We can call the previously created procedure with the following CALL statement:

```
CALL HANA_DEMO."PROC_SALES_REPORT" (8, null);
```

You can see the created procedure below our schema under the **Procedure...** folder.

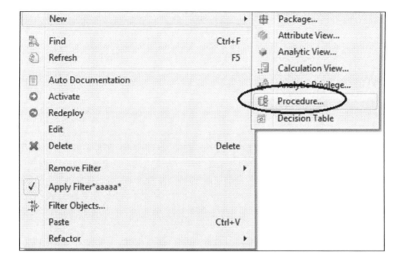

Procedure creation using the wizard

Choose the package in which you want to create the procedure and right-click on it.

A new screen will pop up; fill in the details and click on **Confirm**:

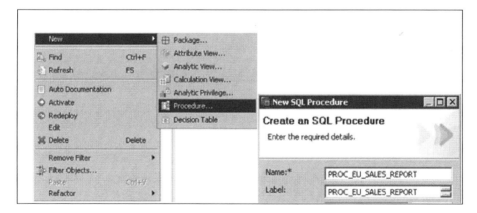

The SQL console opens with default syntax; we need to put our logic in between BEGIN and END.

The following is a sample logic with which I am creating the Procedure:

```
/*********BEGIN PROCEDURE SCRIPT ***********/
BEGIN
Pvar1 = SELECT T1.REGION_NAME, T1.SUB_AREA, T2.PRODUCT_KEY, T2.AMOUNT_SOLD
        FROM AS "HANA_DEMO"."REGION"T1
        INNER JOIN
        "HANA_DEMO"."SALES_FACTS"AS T2
        ON T1.REGION_KEY = T2.REGION_KEY;

Pvar2 = SELECT T1.REGION_NAME, T1.SUB_AREA, T1.PRODUCT_KEY, T1.AMOUNT_SOLD, T2.PRODUCT_NAME
        FROM :Pvar1 AS T1
        INNER JOIN
        "HANA_DEMO"."PRODUCTS"AS T2
        ON T1.PRODUCT_KEY = T2.PRODUCT_KEY;

OUTPUT_TABLE = SELECT SUM(AMOUNT_SOLD) AS AMOUNT_SOLD, SUM(AMOUNT_SOLD - (AMOUNT_SOLD * :DISCOUNT/ 100)) AS NET_AMOUNT,
        PRODUCT_NAME, REGION_NAME, SUB_AREA
        FROM :Pvar2
        GROUP BY PRODUCT_NAME, REGION_NAME, SUB_AREA;
END;
/*********END PROCEDURE SCRIPT ***********/
```

On the left-hand side of the screen, you can see the output pane:

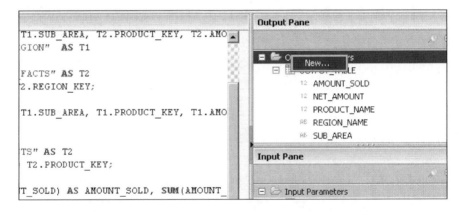

Click on it and select **New...**:

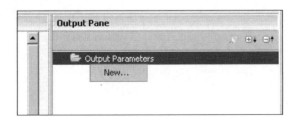

Define the columns which we used in the preceding procedure:

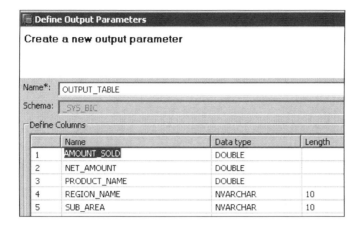

Similarly, perform the same steps for input parameters as well:

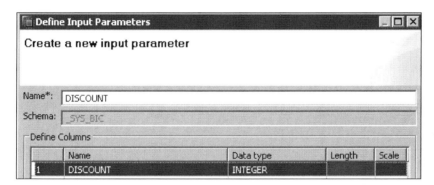

Now the procedure is ready to be called via the `CALL` statement.

Once we build our concept about different views, then one question that will definitely come to our mind is, should we use calculation views (not yet discussed) or procedures. We will discuss this once we have discussed the calculation view in *Chapter 5, Creating SAP HANA Artifacts – Analytical Privileges and Calculation Views*.

JOINS in SAP HANA

To address some specific business cases and have improved execution, SAP HANA introduces some additional JOINS on top of existing SQL JOINS. These SAP HANA specific JOINS are as follows:

- Referential JOIN
- Text JOIN
- Temporal JOIN
- Star JOIN
- Spatial JOIN

Let's see the scenarios when we should consider using these SAP HANA specific JOINS :

Type	Scenario / use case	Remarks
Referential JOIN	Facts with matching dimensions only where referential integrity is ensured.	It's the default join type in SAP HANA. Facts returned are dependent on queried attributes.
Text JOIN	Multi language table.	Needs a language column. Behaves as the left outer join.
Temporal JOIN	A key date within a validity period.	Acts as a referential join.
Star JOIN	Star schema scenarios.	Needs data organized in a star schema. All attributes and hierarchies are included.
Spatial join	Geospatial data.	Only available in calculation views.

Unions versus JOINS

Unions are used to combine the result set of two or more SELECT statements. It's always tempting to JOIN two analytic views when measures from more than one table are required. This should, however, be avoided for performance reasons. It is more beneficial to use a Union in a calculation view. Technically, a Union is not a JOIN type.

Points to remember:

- Union is not supported in the attribute or analytical view but can only be used in calculation views.
- Union with constant values are supported within graphical calculation views and the Union operator can accept 1..N input sources.
- Script-based calculation views can only accept two input sources at a given time.
- Do not JOIN analytical views (to be discussed later), as you might have performance issues. Instead, use Union with constant values when working with multiple fact tables.

Self-study questions

1. What are the other JOINS used in classic SQL that are not mentioned in the preceding discussion, and how are they different?
2. Can you think of use cases where you should use procedure?

Summary

With this chapter, we set the base for the book. It was expected that you already knew these topics and the chapter refreshed them for you. We started with the basics of SQL and how to use SAP HANA SQL statements. We progressed to create SQLscript and procedure. Towards the closure of the chapter, you learned about additional JOINS that SAP HANA has to improve business scenarios, and we closed the chapter with a discussion on Union and JOINS.

In the next chapter, we will cover the approach to SAP HANA data modeling and the dos and don'ts while creating data models. You will also learn which kind of view should be created for different types of information.

2

SAP HANA Data Modeling Approach

This chapter gets you started with the modeling approach. We start with a discussion about row and column storage and their usage. Then, we move on to the architecture of the SAP HANA engine and understand how different views are processed. We will also discuss the different schemas available in SAP HANA. This chapter will introduce you to modeling principle and guidelines. We will perform a comparative study of different modeling artifacts in SAP HANA. We will close the chapter with a learning of the SAP HANA Studio and how to create packages and delivery units.

After completing this chapter, you should be able to:

- Differentiate between row and column storage, and know when to use what
- Understand basic architecture of the SAP HANA engine
- Differentiate between modeling artifacts in SAP HANA
- Know modeling principles
- Learn to use the SAP HANA Studio
- Differentiate schemas in SAP HANA
- Create packages and delivery units

Row and column storage in SAP HANA

Relational databases typically use row-based data storage. SAP HANA uses both (row based and column based data storage)

- **The row storage**: This stores records in a sequence of rows
- **The column storage**: The column entries are stored in a continuous memory location

Before getting into a SAP HANA specific discussion, let's try to understand how different column storage is from row. The column-oriented database systems (in our case, SAP HANA) perform better than traditional row-oriented database systems on analytical tasks, in areas such as data warehouses, decision support, predictive analysis, and business intelligence applications.

The major reason behind this performance difference in these areas is that column stores are more I/O efficient for read-only queries as they only have to read the attributes accessed by a query from the disk or memory.

Let's see a few factors that optimize performance in the column storage:

- **Compression**: The data stored in columns is more compressible as compared to data stored in rows. Compression algorithms perform better on data with low information entropy (high data value locality). A good example could be an employee table (which includes the employee name, number, and e-mail address). Storing data in columns allows all of the names to be stored together, all of the employee numbers together, and so on. Certainly, phone numbers are more similar to each other than the surrounding text fields such as **Name**. Further, if the data is sorted by one of the columns, that column will be super-compressible.

- **Block iteration and support for parallelism**: In the row storage, while processing a series of tuples, it first iterates through each tuple, and then it extracts the needed attributes from these tuples through a tuple representation interface. In contrast to the case-by-case implementation in row and column storage blocks of values from the same column are sent to an operator in a single function call. No attribute extraction is needed, and if the column is fixed-width, these values can be iterated through directly as an array. Operating on data as an array not only minimizes per-tuple overhead, but it also exploits potential for parallelism on CPUs.

- **Late materialization**: In a column store, information about a logical entity is stored in multiple locations on disk, whereas in a row store such information is usually collocated in a single row of a table. However, most queries access more than one attribute from a particular entity. So, at some point in most query plans, data from multiple columns must be combined together into rows of information about an entity. Consequently, this join-like materialization of tuples (also called "tuple construction") is an extremely common operation in a column store.

There are a couple of advantages of late materialization:

° Selection and aggregation operators tend to render the construction of some tuples unnecessary (if the executor waits long enough before constructing a tuple, it might be able to avoid constructing it altogether)

° If data is compressed using a column-oriented compression method, it must be decompressed before the combination of values with values from other columns

It is up to the data modeler in the SAP HANA database to specify whether a table is to be stored column-wise or row-wise. One can also alter an existing column-based table to row-based, and vice versa. Let's take a diagrammatical approach to see how row and column representation happens for a table:

- Logical representation of a Table:

Country	Currency	Sales
DE	€	600
UK	£	100
US	$	400
NL	€	200

- Traditionally data is stored in database as row and can be represented as follows:

DE	€	600	UK	£	100	US	$	400	NL	€	200

- If we use Column based data storage, the representation for the same table would look like as follows:

DE	UK	US	NL	€	£	$	€	600	100	400	200

Having seen the row and column representation, we can clearly correlate the preceding mentioned points of compression, block iteration, parallel processing, and late materialization.

Choosing the right table

It is up to a data modeler in the SAP HANA database to specify whether a table is to be stored column-wise or row-wise. One can also alter an existing column-based table to row-based, and vice versa.

The following figure shows some of the scenarios for using the row and column store:

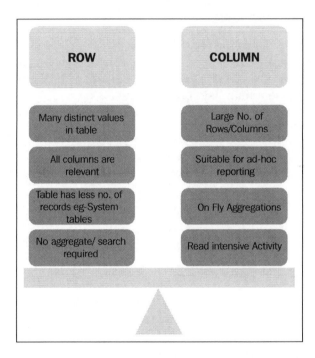

As illustrated in the figure, each store has an advantage in different scenarios and SAP HANA allows you to choose how you want to store your data—row or column as per your need. The SAP HANA database allows joining column table with row table.

Other features of SAP HANA that we should also be aware of are:

- **Partitioning**: In the SAP HANA database, tables can be partitioned horizontally into disjunctive subtables or partitions. Partitioning supports the creation of very large tables by decomposing them into smaller manageable chunks.

Two of the most widely used cases for partitioning are as follows:

- ° **Parallelization**: Operations are parallelized by using several execution threads per table.

- ° **Load balancing**: Using partitioning, the individual partitions might be distributed over the landscape. This way, a query on a table is not processed by a single server but by all the servers that host partitions that are relevant for processing.

- **Insert only on Delta**: The challenge of updating and inserting data into a sorted column store table is huge, as the whole table (sort order) is reorganized each time. SAP has tackled this challenge by separating these tables into main stores (read-optimized, sorted columns) and delta stores (write-optimized, nonsorted columns or rows).

There is a regular database activity that merges the Delta stores into the main store. This activity is called **Delta Merge**.

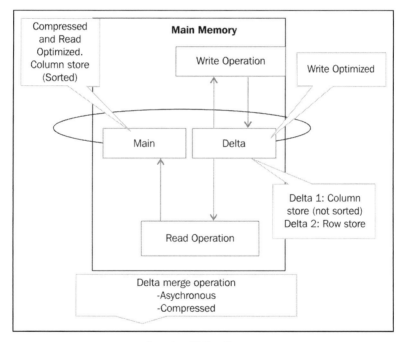

Insert on Delta - Process

Merge process can be understood in three phases. Operation that are performed before Merge, during merge and post Merge.(Steps are illustrated in the preceding diagram).

1. Before the merge operation: All write operations go to storage Delta1 and read operations read from storages Main1 and Delta1.

2. During the merge operation: All the changes go to the second delta storage (Delta 2) While the merge operation is running. Read operations read from the original main storage, Main1, and from both delta storages, Delta1 and Delta 2. Uncommitted changes in Delta 1 are copied to Delta 2. The content of Main1 and the committed entries in Delta 1 are merged into the new main storage, Main2.

3. After the merge operation: Once the merge process is complete . Main1 and Delta 1 storages are deleted.

Basic architecture of the SAP HANA engine

SAP HANA has different engines to process different views. It has the following engines:

*   **JOIN engine**: This engine is for processing the JOINS (all type of joins)/ attribute views

*   **OLAP engine**: This engine is used to process analytical view

*   **CALCULATION engine**: This engine is used to process complex calculation that cannot be processed by the JOIN or OLAP engine

It is the SQL optimizer, which sees the models and queries and decides which engine to call.

Any analytic view or attribute view with a calculate attribute will be processed as a calculation view. This should to be taken into consideration during modeling, because it can have a measurable impact on the performance of the data model. Different engines cooperate among themselves as well.

The following figure shows the SAP HANA engines processing different views:

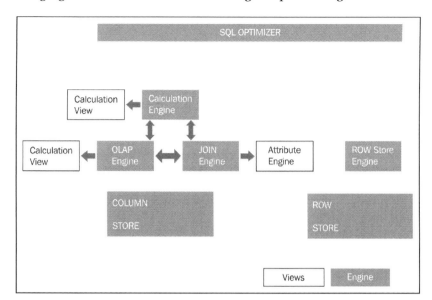

Other than the preceding illustrated engines, we do have a planning engine as well in SAP HANA. The planning engine, allows financial planning applications to execute basic planning operations in the database layer. For example, one such basic operation is to create a new version of a dataset as a copy of an existing one while applying filters and transformations.

Different modeling artifacts in SAP HANA

Before creating a new SAP HANA modeling artifact it is of paramount importance to know which types of modeling artifacts will be suitable for our business need. Depending on the scenario you are working in, your choice might vary. Factors that should be taken into consideration are:

- The write- or read-intensive scenario, so as to decide between column and row storage
- Data access need and resources for the replication method available
- The application or client to be supported with your information model as different clients expose/consume data differently
- Performance and functionality, as not all views can give the same functionality or performance

The first thing we need to decide is do we need a column table or row store. Once we have decided, we can have a glance at the following table and choose the views, if our requirement can be fulfilled by any of these:

	Column table	Analytical view	Calculation view (SQL)	Calculation view (CE function)
Scenario	This is simple and good for demo / to start with use case.	As the name suggests, this is for analytical scenarios where read on mass data is needed.	This is simple and for scenarios with few fields to quickly build models for complex calculations.	This is useful for complex calculation cases where an analytical view cannot be useful.
Pro	This is easy to consume. No additional modeling required.	This is Optimized, we can model it as per our need and It is optimized for select statements.	This is an easy syntax, as most of us are well versed with SQL.	This is well optimized and parallelized. In most cases, it performs better than SQL.
Cons	This is low on performance as there is heavy logic performed on the client side. Many features are not supported (analytical privilege).	This has limited functionality.	This is not always the most optimized query, and it is slower than other models.	There are different syntax, which are new for most of us.

Modeling principles

The following illustration shows the various considerations that we should be aware of and we should consider –avoid transfer of large result sets, and so on during HANA modeling. The idea is to filter the data at the lowest layer and only bring in data that is actually required by the query.

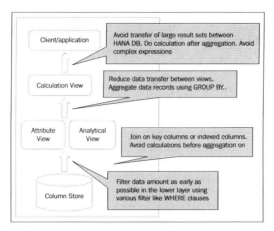

Modeling Principles – consideration to make

The following decision tree can help us decide which view to use or what artifacts we should model. You can start with the very requirement and follow the decision tree flowchart to drill to what view you should use:

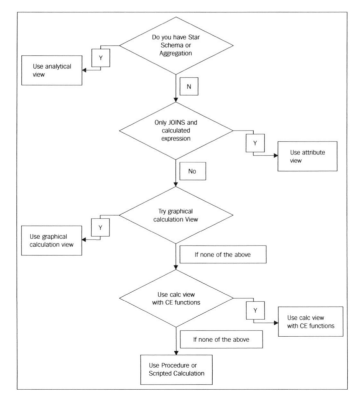

A flowchart to help you to choose the appropriate view

When deciding which views will be most efficient for your information model, it is recommended to follow the decision tree as a guide to identify the views you want to create based on analysis of requirements. For the best performance and ease of maintenance, it is beneficial to stay on the top three levels of the decision tree whenever possible.

We will discuss view-specific recommendation in *Chapter 4, Creating SAP HANA Artifacts Attribute Views and Analytical Views*, when we discuss each view in detail.

SAP HANA Studio

The SAP HANA Studio is a client tool to connect to the SAP HANA database. It is a Java-based application that runs on the Eclipse platform. It is delivered as part of the SAP HANA installation package, and provides an environment for administration, modeling, development, and data provisioning.

We will be primarily working with SAP HANA Studio for all our modeling needs in this book.

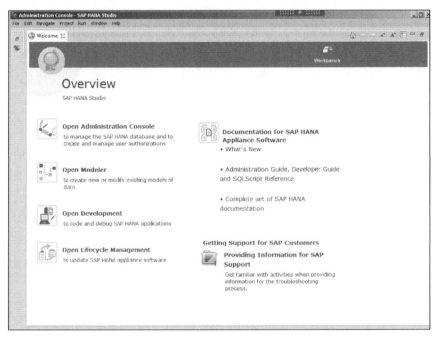

SAP HANA Studio

Perspectives in SAP HANA Studio

Perspectives are predefined user interface layouts with several views. We have the following perspectives:

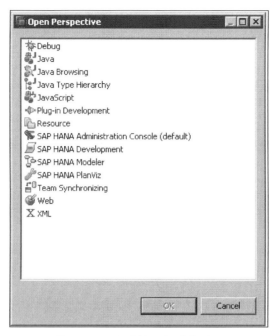

Perspectives in SAP HANA Studio

Let's see a few of the perspectives and their usage in detail:

- **SAP HANA Administration Console**: This perspective is used by SAP HANA administrators to administrate and monitor the whole SAP HANA system. We will use it to add our system to the SAP HANA instance into SAP HANA Studio.

- **SAP HANA Modeler**: The SAP HANA Modeler perspective is used by data modeler to create information models and data artifacts, as a combination of attributes, dimensions, and measures, included in different types of modelling views.

There are other perspectives as well such as Resource, JAVA, and so on for other specific usages.

If you get lost while traversing different perspectives, you can always go to the **Menu** option and choose **Window Reset Perspective** to return to the default view and perspective.

Adding our system to SAP HANA Studio

Before we can start using SAP HANA Studio, we need to add our SAP HANA instance to the studio. The following are the steps to do so:

1. Open **SAP HANA Administrative Console** from the default studio screen.

2. In **Systems View** (at the right-hand side of the studio layout), right-click in the blank space and choose **Add System...**, as illustrated in the following screenshot:

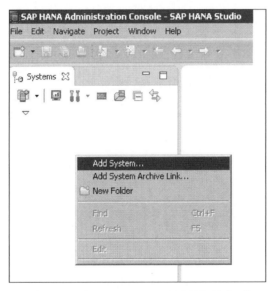

Adding a SAP HANA system to SAP HANA Studio

An alternate step to add a system is by clicking on the **Add System...** icon in **Systems View** and choosing **Add System**.

3. Provide details such as **Host Name**, **Instance Number**, and **Description**, as shown in the following screenshot:

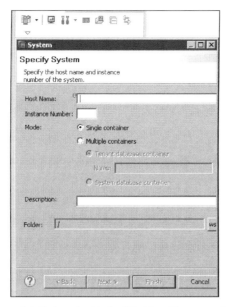

Server details (required to be filled to add your system)

4. It then asks for user credentials, provide it as given/created:

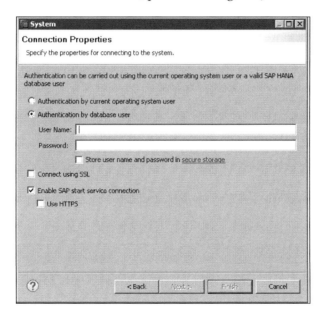

The user with which the system would be added to SAP HANA studio.

The system view

This displays the main part of the SAP HANA system as a folder structure. For each system that you add to your HANA Studio, the content will be organized as shown in the following screenshot:

Folder structures in the system view in SAP HANA Studio

Depending upon your role provided to you by your security team you might see backup structures in the system view in SAP HANA Studio:

- **Catalog**: This contains tables, views, indexes, and so on. All these objects are organized into schemas

- **Content**: This stores all SAP HANA specific modeling objects

- **Provisioning**: The **Provisioning** folder is related to **Smart Data Access**, a data provisioning approach in which you can combine data from remote sources (such as Hadoop, SAP ASE) with the data of your SAP HANA physical tables, by exposing them as virtual tables

- **Security**: Users and roles in the system are stored here

- **Backup**: Depending upon your role, you might see an additional backup folder, which contains information about Backups

Different schemas in SAP HANA

Schemas are used to categorize database content according to customer defined groupings that have a particular meaning for users. Schemas also help to define access rights to the database objects. Schemas can help identify which tables to use when defining information models. But a model can incorporate tables from multiple schemas, which are:

- System defined

- User defined

- SLT derived schemas

System defined schemas are delivered with the SAP HANA database and contain the HANA system's information. These are system schemas such as _SYS_BIC, _SYS_BI, _SYS_REPO, _SYS_STATISTICS, and so on.

Let's see more about these system defined schemas:

- _SYS_BIC: This schema contains all the column views of activated objects. When the user activates any of the views, say the attribute view/analytical view / the calculation view, the respective runtime objects are created under the _SYS_BIC column view.

- _SYS_REPO: This contains a list of activated objects, inactive objects, package details, and runtime object's information and so on. The objects that are in the system are available in this repository.

- _SYS_BI: This schema stores all the metadata of created column views. It contains the table for created variables, time data (fiscal and geographical), schema mapping, and content mapping tables.

- _SYS_STATISTICS: This contains all the system configuration and parameters.

- _SYS_XS: This is used for SAP HANA extended application services.

Points to remember while working with schema:

- Schema layouts should be planned before you start your project.

- There is no standard naming convention for naming schemas but giving generic names to schemas helps. For example, SLT_<SID> for SLT schema from a source (<SID>) and CUST_SCHEMA for customer schema.

- Try to maintain the same names of schemas in the DEV/QAS/PROD environment. This helps while migrating modeling content from one environment to the other. Different names create unnecessary confusion and adjustment each time you move the content.

- Keep separate schemas for staging tables, custom tables, and also consider the method of replication (separate schema for SLT/DS).

Creating package and delivery unit

Package is a repository used to organize various modeling artifacts along with other modeling objects such as analytical privileges and procedures. It is assigned to a delivery unit so as to transport the objects it contains to another environment.

We can create a package as illustrated in the following screenshot:

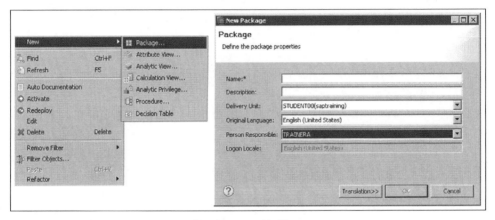

Creating a new Package

Points to remember while creating a new package:

- Create one top-level package for all of the customer's content (if acceptable to the customer).

- Create a subpackage for the content you will deploy in the project. This could be on the basis of different scrum teams or application areas.

- Multiple subpackages might be created, if required or desired, to organize a large amount of content.

- Create one top-level package called dev (or development) for work in progress.

- Create a subpackage for each developer such as task in SAP R/3.

- Create all analytical and calculation views under these play area packages.

- Once the development is complete (including unit testing), these views can be copied/moved to the main package for the project when it is ready to migrate between environments. Always take backups (exporting content) of the entire content of a project.

- Many customers use perforce or other tools, or one can also use the HANA repository to check in or out.

- For version management, instead of using the Developer mode to export and import, we can use the SAP HANA development perspective to track the version of the objects.

Deleting packages

A package cannot be deleted when it is not empty. Delete all the underlying objects before deleting the package. This includes subpackages.

 Note that some objects are hidden in the modeler perspective. Use the HANA development perspective to see all of the associated objects (also you can change preferences to see hidden objects).

Delivery units

A delivery unit in SAP HANA is used to realize migration of different packages from different environments (landscapes). A delivery unit could be regarded as a collection of several packages for centralization of management.

Let's see how can we create a Delivery Units.

In the quick view, you can see the tab for **Delivery Units**. Click on it as shown in the following screenshot:

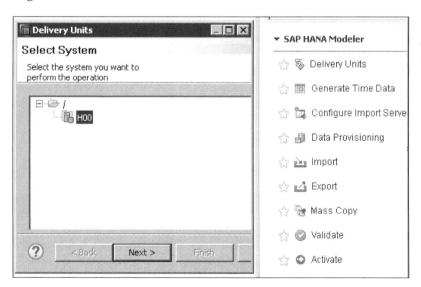

Creating a delivery unit

This will ask you to choose a system. Once you choose the appropriate system and instance (here we have only one, you might have multiple in the productive environment), click on **Next**. It will enlist all the existing delivery units and an option to add new, as shown in the following screenshot:

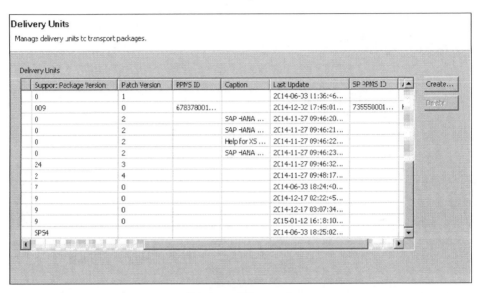

Creating a delivery unit

Since we want to create a new delivery unit, we click on **Create...** and it pops up a new screen where you have to fill the details:

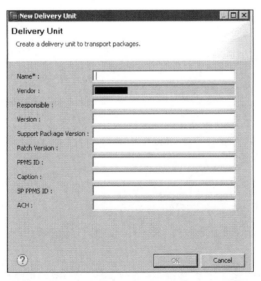

Please fill in the details for creating a delivery unit

Points to remember while creating a delivery unit, which can be of help:

- Create a delivery unit for each group of related content that you will deploy for the project
- This will be used for migrating your content from DEV to QA and PROD
- In general, the delivery units should match the subpackages under the top-level package for the customer
- Assign your deployment packages (under the top-level customer package) to the appropriate delivery units

Self-study questions

1. Will you create a row table or column table if you have a table on which you perform an equal number of read and write operations? What factors will you consider in such scenarios?
2. Can a delivery unit or package be modified into a non-original system, that is, a delivery unit created in system S and migrated to system P, can it be modified in system P?

Summary

In this chapter, you learned the difference between row and column storage and when to use what. You got an insight of how we can have better analytics with help of column based tables. We discussed the basic architecture of the SAP HANA engine, which helped you understand which view would be processed in which engine. Later, we also did a comparative study of different modeling artifacts in SAP HANA. Modeling principle and guideline were also outlined with a brief on the different schemas available in SAP HANA. At the end of the chapter, you learned about SAP HANA Studio and a step-by-step way of creating package and delivery unit.

In the next chapter, you will learn how to load data into SAP HANA, explore various options of data load as per the data source, and understand real-time replication via SLT. You will learn how to use SAP HANA Studio and will have a quick look at the SAP business object data service and SAP direct extractor for data load.

Different Ways of SAP HANA Data Load

3

In the previous chapter, you got an understanding of the approach that we should take for data modeling and learned about various artifacts in SAP HANA. In this chapter, we detail the key data load methods and the technical components that enable data loading in SAP HANA. In this book, we will not be talking about data loading in a SAP BW or any other system running on HANA database. Rather, we will keep the discussion focused on SAP HANA as standalone system.

After completing this chapter, you should be able to:

- Load data from Flat file in SAP HANA
- Understand the concept of real-time replication via SAP LT
- Work with SAP HANA Studio for data provisioning
- Load data with Direct Extractor
- Load data with SAP Business Object Data Services Workbench
- Understand how SAP Replication Server and Smart Data Access works

Before we start to create information models, we need to import all the required table definitions and load the tables with data in SAP HANA. Different data load techniques have their own prerequisites. For example, if **Systems Landscape Transformation (SLT)** is used, the basis administrator has to configure the schemas for the source system and target system (SAP HANA, in this case) during installation. Let's look at the various available and popular data load methods in some SAP HANA sidecar scenarios.

We will discuss the following data provisioning techniques in this book:

- Uploading data from Flat file
- SAP Landscape Transformation Replication Server
- The SAP Direct Extractor Connection
- SAP Business Object Data Services Workbench
- SAP Replication Server
- Smart Data Access

Loading data from Flat file in SAP HANA

Prior to Revision 28 (SPS04) of SAP HANA Studio, loading data from flat file was a tedious task. Users had to use SAP Information Composer or go into a complex process of creating a control file, moving the files to server, and then executing SQL scripts to load the data. With **Data from Local File** in SAP HANA Studio (SPS04, rev28 and above), it takes just a few mouse clicks to upload data into SAP HANA from files that have CSV, XLS, or XLSX extensions.

Try to understand this step-by-step using an example. We have an XLS file that contains sales data for xyz customer and we need this data in SAP HANA.

	Clipboard			Font	
	E18			f_x	
	A	B	C	D	E
1	Country	Currency	Sales		
2	DE	$	600		
3	UK	$	100		
4	US	$	400		
5	NL	$	200		
6					

* common currency ($) is used irrespective of country

We will proceed as follows:

1. Open SAP HANA Studio | **Quick Launch** | **Content Section** | **Import** | **SAP HANA Content** | **Data from Local File**.

2. Choose **Data from Local File** and click **Next**.

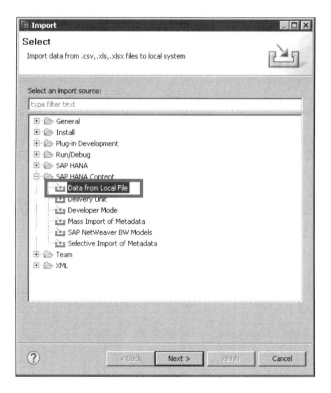

3. You will be prompted to select **Target System** (where the data will be imported), so choose choose the system, the target system, where you want to import the data and click **Next**.

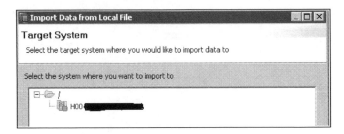

4. The following screen appears and allows you to set the properties of **Import**, such as **Target Table** and New Schema.

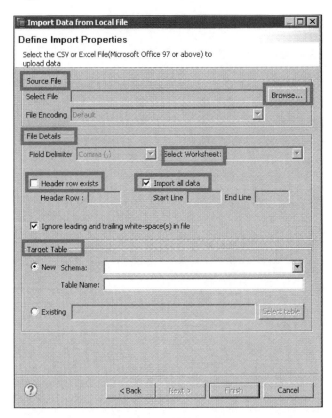

As you can see in the preceding screen capture, you are not only asked to give the path of the source CSV/XLS/XLSX, but you have the option of setting other properties as well. The list of properties is explained as follows:

° **Source File**: Click on **Browse** and choose Flat file you want to upload.

° **Field Delimiter**: This option is for multi-sheet Excel documents where you can select from a different worksheet. Examples of Field Delimiter - comma, Semicolon, or colon.

° **Select Worksheet**: Your Excel/CSV file might have multiple worksheets, so this tab allows you to choose the one you want to load. This option is greyed out if the file has only one worksheet.

° **Import all data**: This tab helps you to choose and decide how much data you want to load. Do you want to upload everything or from a particular line to some other line.

° **Header row exists**: If your source file has header row defined, you need to check this box. Otherwise just leave it unchecked.

° **Target Table, New/Existing**: You choose whether you want to load data in a new table or existing table. If you choose new, you need to specify the schema where it should be created and give a name to table. The existing option is used when you want to append data into existing table.

Fill all the relevant fields with data, as follows:

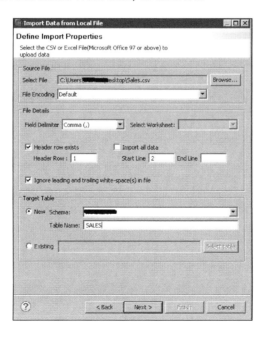

5. Since we are loading data from an Excel sheet and Excel does not contains the data types and primary/secondary key concept, this method of data loading facilitates a feature where we can define the data type and key before loading it into SAP HANA.

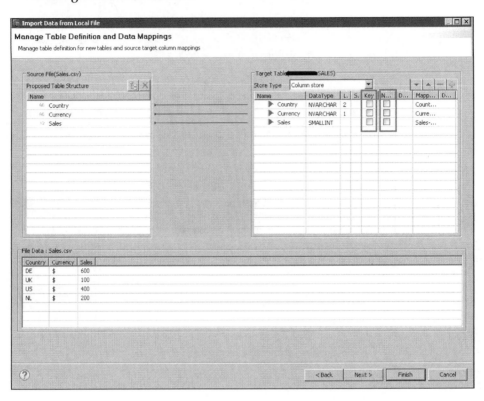

6. We will make **Country** field as **Key** and also make it NOT NULL.

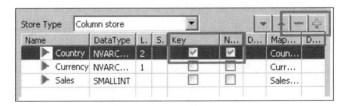

7. The interface before loading asks for a final confirmation and review.

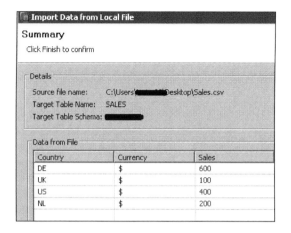

8. On confirmation, the process is complete and we can go to SAP HANA Studio to see the table under the relevant schema, as shown in the following screenshot:

9. We can also do a data preview to validate that the data load was successful and the data at source and data in here (Data Preview) are same.

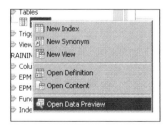

10. We can see the same data in SAP HANA as was in the Excel sheet at the start.

	Name	SQL Data Type	Di...	Column Store Data Type	Key	Not Null	Defau
1	Country	NVARCHAR	2	STRING	X(1)	X	
2	Currency	NVARCHAR	1	STRING			
3	Sales	SMALLINT		INT			

Table Name: SALES Schema: ▬▬▬▬ Type: Column Store

Columns | Indexes | Further Properties | Runtime Information

This completes the end-to-end data load via flat file upload. The data loaded via this mechanism is not real time and is static in nature. In next section, you will learn the concept of real-time data loading/replication and explore how it works.

Real-time replication via SAP SLT (System Landscape Transformation) Replication Server

SLT Replication Server is positioned for real-time data replication from SAP and non-SAP sources (SAP supported data bases only). It also provides the ability to perform complex data transformations on the fly. It is mainly recommended for real-time data replication business scenarios.

The replication mechanism of SAP SLT is focused on trigger-based replication functionalities. It uses delta processes for replication. Let's see the various components used in SAP LT Server. The following is the diagrammatical representation of SLT server for SAP and non-SAP sources.

The following diagram shows the various components of the SAP system landscape transformation setup:

- When the source system is SAP:

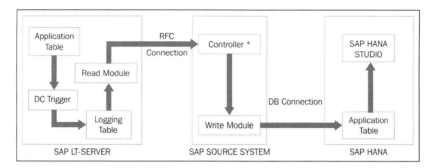

- When the source is a non-SAP system

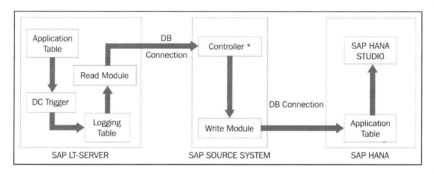

Let's look at each components one by one:

- **DB trigger**: This is the code that updates a database automatically in response to a certain event. For replication, it should be a marker.
- **Logging table**: This is a table in the source system that records any changes to a table that is being replicated. It keeps track and ensures that SLT Replication Server can replicate these changes to the target system.
- **Application table**: The relevant data is read from the application tables (source).
- **Read Module**: Read modules transfer the data from the source system to the SAP LT.
- **Replication Server**: If the source is SAP, then it's located on the SAP source system; otherwise it's on the replication server in the case of a non-SAP source system.

- **Controller**: This is used for structure mapping and transformation.
- **RFC connection**: If the source is SAP, the RFC connection between the SAP source system and SAP LT Replication Server has to be established.
- **DB connection**: For non-SAP sources, we need establish the database connection by using a transaction DBCO in SAP LT Replication Server.

Some silent features of SAP LT are:

- Real-time data replication, if required it can be scheduled with SAP SLT, you can replicate the data real time or you can schedule it (non real-time)
- Data formatting (SAP HANA specific) need not require a separate step, as it's done during the replication step only
- Supports all releases from SAP R/3 4.6C and above
- Non-unicode to unicode conversion is supported automatically during loading/replication
- Filtering of data, formatting table structure, and hiding fields is possible if required
- It is completely integrated with SAP HANA Studio
- It has extended monitoring capabilities if used in conjunction with SAP Solution Manager 710 SPS05 and above

SAP LT has various use case scenarios, and some of the popular usages are:

- Used with SAP HANA Studio for SAP HANA sidecar application
- Used for real-time data acquisition for SAP BW
- Used as application accelerators for RDS solutions for data mart
- Other project-based specific scenarios

 Prerequisite: The source system and target schema needs to be configured by the administrator during installation.

Let's see how a SLT Replication can be triggered via SAP HANA Studio.
The step-by-step SLT replication are as follows:

1. In the **Quick View** pane, choose **Data Provisioning....**

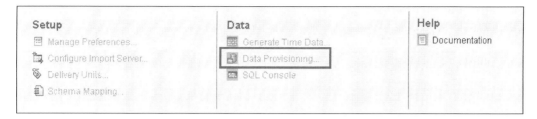

2. Select a system where you want to perform this operation.

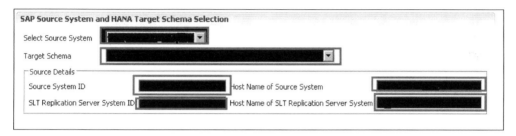

   - In the preceding screen, choose one of the source systems from the **Select Source System** drop-down list (the **Select Source System** drop-down list contains all the ERP and non-ERP source systems that are connected to the SLT system).

   - Choose the schema, in the target system, where you want the tables to be replicated.

3. From the following options, choose the appropriate option as per your requirements. Choose **Load** for the initial load or **Replicate** for data replication.

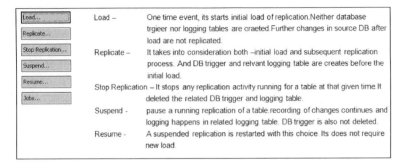

Load –	One time event, its starts initial load of replication.Neither database trgieer nor logging tables are craeted.Further changes in source DB after load are not replicated.
Replicate –	It takes into consideration both –initial load and subsequent replication process. And DB trigger and relvant logging table are creates before the initial load.
Stop Replication –	It stops any replication activity running for a table at that given time It deleted the related DB trigger and logging table.
Suspend -	pause a running replication of a table.recording of changes continues and logging happens in related logging table. DB trigger is also not deleted.
Resume -	A suspended replication is restarted with this choice. Its does not require new load.

Use **Suspend** if you just want momentarily stop replication; otherwise you will have to reload the whole table again. You should not suspend replication of a table for long period as it will create a huge (size) logging table.

4. Select the required tables to load or replicate data in any of the following ways:

    ◦   Search for the required tables

    ◦   Select the table from the list and choose **Add**

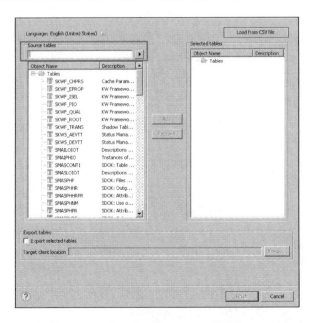

If you have N number of tables to be loaded / replicated, then creating a list in a file and loading it would be an easier way. Load the list of tables from a local file as follows:

- ° Choose **Load from file**
- ° Select the file that contains the required list of tables (the supported file type is .csv)
- ° If you are using the load controller infrastructure, choose **Next** and enter the operating system username and password.
- ° Choose **Finish**

5. Select the **Export selected tables** checkbox if you want to save the selected list of tables locally for future reference, and specify the target location.

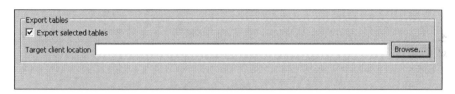

6. Over a period of time, the SAP HANA status tables grow very large with data load action status entries that do not need to be maintained. You can choose to delete these entries from the SAP HANA status tables using the **Delete** button in the Data Load Management view. Once you choose this option in the follow-on dialog, you can select which entries you want to delete in the status tables.

7. Choose the operation where you want to delete the status table entries such as load, replicate, or create.

8. In the **Entry Type** drop-down list, select the required option.

9. Please keep following points in mind while deleting entries:

- ° To delete all the entries from the status tables for a particular operation, choose **All**, otherwise **Specific**.
- ° If the value for **Entry Type** is **Specific** in the Value dropdown list, select the tables for which you want to delete the entries.
- ° If you want to delete the entries for a specific time period, select it using the **From** and **To** calendar options.

10. Choose **Delete**.

Replication/loading can also be triggered from the LT Replicate Server cockpit in SLT Server. The steps to do so are:

1. Log in to your SLT server with the required authorization.

2. Run the t-code LTRC. You get the LT cockpit.

3. Choose **Data Provisioning**.

4. Enter the table name and choose load / replicate or the relevant activity you want to do.

This diagram shows the steps:

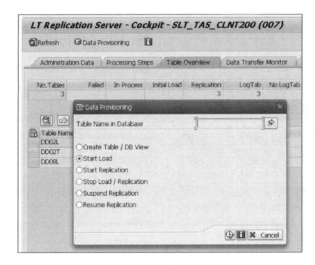

Loading data with SAP Direct Extractor

DXC (Direct Extractor) is a batch-driven data acquisition technique, and a form of extracting, transforming, and loading (ETL) data though its transformation capabilities are limited to user exit for extraction.

The main idea behind DXC is to use existing data models, thereby lowering the **Total cost of Ownership (TCO)**.

Some of the salient features of DXC are:

- Leverage pre-existing foundational data models of SAP Business Suite

- Significantly reduces the complexity of data modeling tasks in SAP HANA

- Reduces the timelines for SAP HANA implementation projects

- Provides semantically rich data from SAP Business Suite to SAP HANA

- Many of the extractors have already got built in application logic to give the data the appropriate contextual meaning
- Reuses an existing proprietary extraction, transformation, and loading mechanism
- it is built into SAP Business Suite systems over a simple HTTP(s) connection to SAP HANA
- No additional server or application is needed in the system landscape
- Provides a mechanism to properly handle data from a delta processing technique

The Step to set up SAP HANA Direct Extractor connection is done in two parts:

1. Importing the DXC relevant Delivery Unit in to SAP HANA.
2. Application server configuration.

Prerequiste: You must have access (Permission) to the directory path `/user/sap/` the server.

3. In the **Modeler** perspective go to quick view | **Import...**:

4. **Import** | **SAP HANA Content** | select **Delivery Unit** | **Next**.

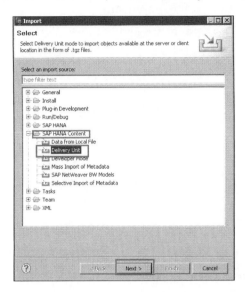

5. Select the server and then provide the patch where you have kept the delivery unit (the default is /usr/sap/HDB/SYS/global/hdb/content).

If we want, we can take it from the client and also by browsing to the local client. Choose HANA_DXC.tgz and click on **Finish**.

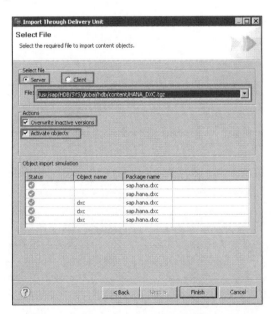

Application server configuration

We need to define the DXC settings in the Xengine service on the master index server's host. To do so, follow these steps:

1. In SAP Hana Studio, go to | **Administrative console** | **Configuration** tab | **xs engine.ini** | **application_container**.

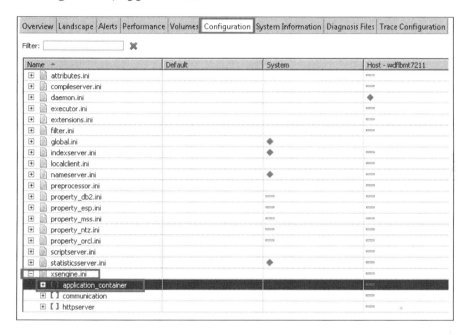

2. Expand **application_container**, then right-click on **application_list**. Click **Change...**.

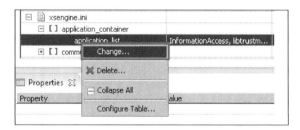

3. In the **System** screen, check for new value field and check that `libxsdxc` is present; otherwise manually add it and click on **Save**.

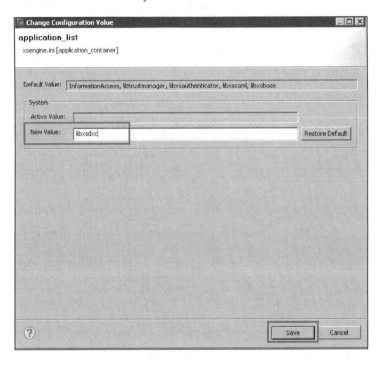

4. After making the changes, you will see a green dot next to **application_list**.

5. You can test the DXC connection application by running the URL:

   `http:/<hostname>/:80<instance number>/sap/hana/dxc/dxc.xscfunc.`

Creating a DXC schema and user in SAP HANA

We will be required to create a unique schema for each specific SAP Business Suite system that we connect to the SAP HANA system with DXC.

1. Go to the **SQL** console in SAP HANA Studio and create the schema:

```
SQL
/**** create schema <schemaname> owned by <dxcusername> ****/
create schema DXCSCHEMA ownedby DXCADMIN; |
```

2. Also create a user via the SQL command in SAP HANA Studio or HANA Studio's graphical interface (**Security** | **Users**).

> Details of other DXC-related configurations and settings can be found at http://help.sap.com/hana/sap_hana_direct_extractor_connection_implementation_guide_en.pdf.

Loading data in SAP HANA with Data Services Workbench

SAP Data Services is an all-in-one solution for data integration. It helps customers with various information management capabilities such as ETL, profiling, text analytics, and metadata management.

Up until now, before Data Service Workbench was introduced, we used to perform the following steps for data loading in SAP HANA via Data Services: Import **Metadata** into **Data Services Workbench** (source system HANA relevant) | create DS jobs to push data in SAP HANA | schedule/run the DS job | data is then available in the relevant schema in SAP HANA.

With Data Services Workbench, the job is much simpler, and we will focus on it here. Data Services Workbench is a new feature and was released with Data Services 4.1. It's part of the installation package for Data services 4.1.

Data Load with SAP Data Services Workbench

These are the steps to set up data provisioning in HANA using Data Services Workbench:

 Source Database setting | Test the connection | Select the tables | Target the database setting | Test the connection | Choose the runtime repository | Execute the replication job.

1. Log in with your CMS credentials:

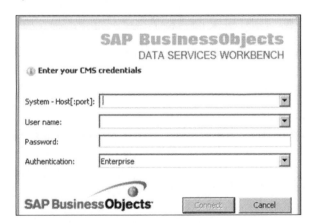

2. Start the replication wizard to see how we can create a data load job:

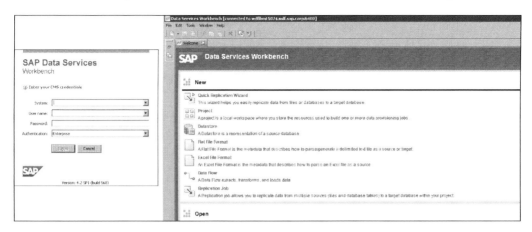

We need to check whether we need metadata along with our data or only data load would fulfill my requirement. Data cannot be loaded until we already have the metadata in the schema. This wizard can be used for both. You should load the meta data first if it's missing.

3. In the next screen, we need to give a project name:

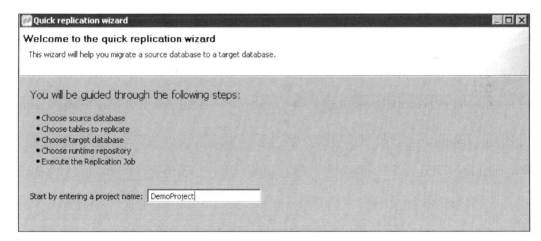

4. Press **Next** to continue.

5. We then have to select our source. SAP data services workbench supports the following as a source:

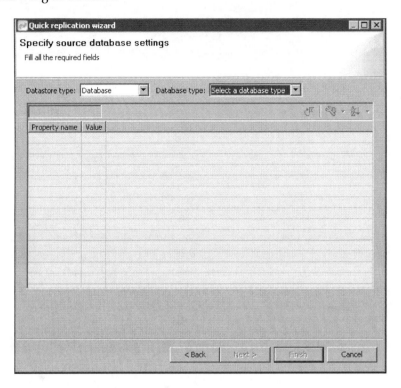

6. We choose SAP HANA as the source.

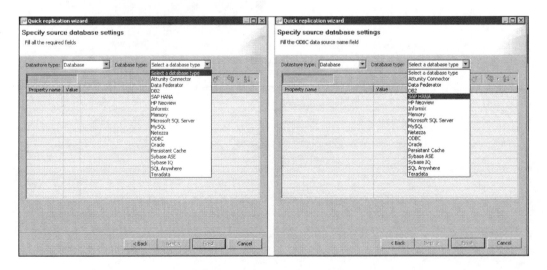

7. We will be required to provide connection credentials once we have selected our database:

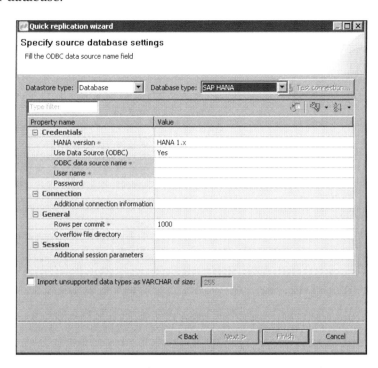

8. Perform a connection test with the following icon:

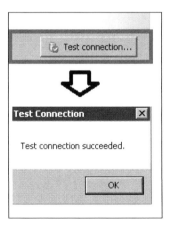

9. Select all the tables you would like to use. You will have a list of tables to select from, which are the tables that are available from the source.

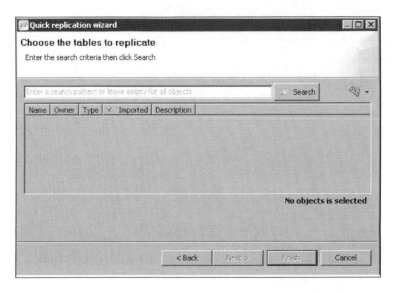

10. The same as with the source, we need to repeat the steps for the target connection. We can only choose from the following three options as a target database:

- ° HANA
- ° Sybase IQ
- ° Teradata

Choose the target DataBase - SAP HANA as shown in the following screenshot:

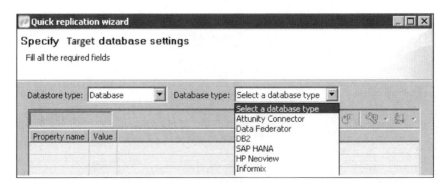

11. Please make a selection for repository and select a server on which the replication job should runs.

    When you're done, you'll get a message saying:

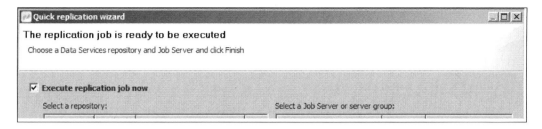

12. Please make a selection for the repository and server on which the replication job should runs.

13. The execution details will be shown in the monitoring part and we can check the table the status to see the data loading be completed.

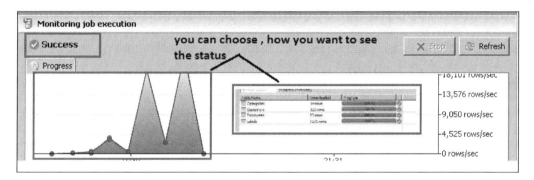

SAP Replication Server

Lets see in brief about another tools from SAP for Data Load. We will not go in detail but have quick look at the basic features and concepts of SAP Replication Server. SAP Replication Server is a log-based database replication tool, and can be used to provision data into a SAP HANA database. The salient features of SAP Replication Server are:

- Bidirectional replication is possible with a standby database always available for read-only reports
- It supports multisite availability, and distributes and synchronizes data across the globe to multiple systems
- Multipath replication is supported from ASE and Oracle

- it supports direct load (no materialization queues are created) to get a better performance

- There is real-time availability of application data to reporting servers and data warehouses

- It enables high availability and disaster recovery for global enterprises

- It migrates data to new databases, hardware, or OS platforms

- Since it works on a log-based mechanism, its performance is very high without disruption

The Main steps to set up Replication using SAP Replication server are:

1. Create the connection to the primary ASE database and HANA database.

2. Create a table in the primary ASE database and mark it for Replication.

3. Create a table in the replicated HANA database.

4. Create replication definition (A replication definition describes the source table to Replication Server, specifying the columns you wantto copy. It may also describe attributes of the destination table. Destination tables that match the specified characteristics can subscribe to the replication definition).

Smart Data Access

SAP HANA Smart Data Access enables easy access to remote data, without copying the data into SAP HANA, so it feels like you are accessing a local table in SAP HANA.

Data Access helps to integrate data from multiple systems in real time regardless of where the data is located. With SDA, you can create virtual tables in SAP HANA that point to remote tables in different data sources, giving complete operatiability to these tables via SQL queries. The following diagram explains the flexibility and operatabilty of SAP SDA:

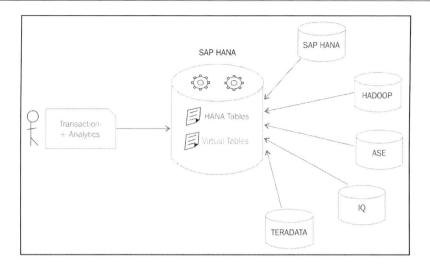

SAP HANA Smart Data Access supports the following databases (as of SAP HANA SP08):

- Oracle 12c, Microsoft SQL Server 2012, Teradata ver13,14, IBM DB2 UDB ver10.1, and Netezza ver7
- Sybase IQ: versions 15.4 ESD#3 and 16.0
- SAP Sybase Adaptive Service Enterprise: version 15.7 ESD#4
- SAP Sybase ESP 5.1 SP04
- Apache Hive 0.9.0. or higher and the Simba HiveODBC driver
- SAP HANA (BW on HANA, Suite on HANA)

For details on how to install the drivers for the databases supported by SAP HANA Smart Data Access, see SAP note 1868702 SAP HANA Smart Data Access: remote data source drivers.

There are some parameter settings that have been made available for SAP HANA Smart Data Access in SAP HANA Studio under **Configuration | indexserver | Smart_Data_Access**. These parameters are for use only by SAP support users and are not meant for end user access.

Now let's try our hand at adjusting the **Parameter Settings** and adding add a remote system for Smart Data Access.

Let's first change the parameter settings for SDA.

1. Go to the **Provisioning** tab of the **Systems** view in SAP HANA Studio:

2. Click on **Smart Data Access**, and a new screen appears as follows:

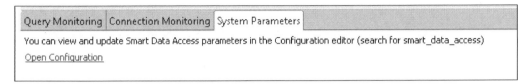

3. Choose **System Parameters**. Then choose to open **Configuration**, which takes you to the **Configuration** tab of **Administrative console**, and apply a filter of **smart_data_access**:

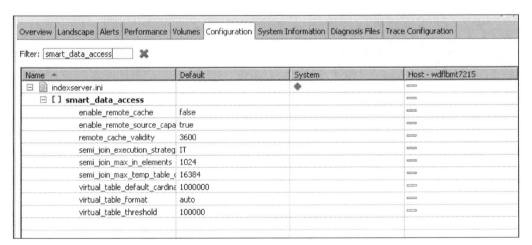

Now we are done with the parameter settings and are good to try our next configuration, adding a remote source.

> It is a prerequisite that you need to configure your ODBC files to the external data source of your choosing.

You can set up a connection to that source in Studio by doing the following (we are using Oracle in our example). The steps to add a remote source are:

1. In your HANA Studio system view, expand your system and go to | **Provisioning** | **Remote Source**.

2. Right-click on the `Remote Sources` folder and select **New Remote Source....**

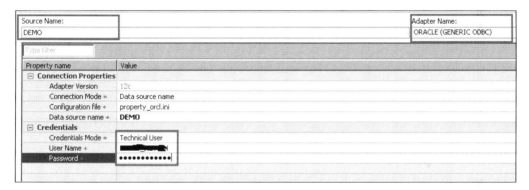

3. The main window pane will request you to enter in the connection information.

4. Click on the **Adapter Name** drop-down and select the appropriate adapter (for this example, we will select Oracle). The main window pane will request you to enter in the connection information as shown in the following screenshot.

5. Press the execute button to save this connection:

6. As an alternative, you can create a remote source through SQL using the following command:

```
CREATE REMOTE SOURCE <Name>ADAPTER "odbc" CONFIGURATION FILE
'property_orcl.ini' CONFIGURATION 'DSN=<DSNNAME>' WITH CREDENTIAL
TYPE 'PASSWORD' USING 'user=<USERNAME>;password=<Password>';
```

7. Press the test connection button to verify that the connection to the source is successful.

8. Under **Remote Source**, you will now see your connection.

After creating the parameters and new resource source, the next task is to access virtual tables.

Let's see how we can access them. The following steps explain how to access them:

1. Traverse to the newly created remote source in your system view.

2. After adding your new remote source, expand it to see the users and the tables.

3. Right-click on the table you would like to access and select **Add as Virtual Table**.

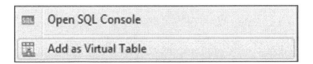

4. You will then choose the alias name and schema you would like to add this virtual table to.

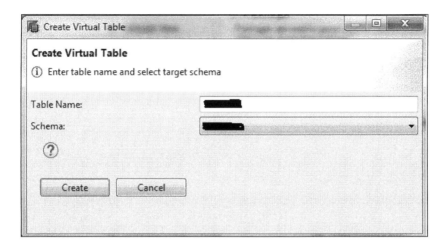

5. Click on **Create**. You will get a confirmation message displaying a message that the virtual table is added to the schema. We can check the schema, and the table would have symbol before it.

6. If you select **Open Definition**, you will see under the **Type,** it says **Virtual.**

Self-study questions

1. Justify the statement – HANA bulk loading is fully report-ready data.

2. How will a partitioning strategy impact data load performance on a single node system and scale out appliance?

Summary

In this chapter, you learned about the different data loading methods and salient features of each. We started the chapter with the simplest method of uploading via flat file and then progressed to real-time replication. One of the major time-consuming activities in reporting is data loading, so choosing the right method as per your requirements and infrastructure becomes of paramount importance. You learned about all the available tools and methods that can be used or are being used. On one side, you learned about Smart Data Access, which gave us the concept of virtual tables without actually copying data into SAP HANA. On the other side, you saw how SAP Replication Server helps with multisite availability using log-based replication. We also showed you in detail how SLT works and can be used for real-time replication.

In the next chapter, you will learn how to create HANA artifacts—attribute view and analytical view. You will learn about various other components involved during the creation of these artifacts. These artifacts will use the data that is loaded using the techniques that you learned about in this chapter.

4

Creating SAP HANA Artifacts Attribute Views and Analytical Views

Now that we have loaded the data into SAP HANA with the key data load methods and the technical components that we learned in *Chapter 3, Different Ways of SAP HANA Data Load*, we move to the next step in this chapter and learn how to create HANA artifacts: attribute view and analytical view. We will also walk through various other components involved during creation of these artifacts. These artifacts will use the data that gets loaded with the techniques that we learned about in *Chapter 3, Different Ways of SAP HANA Data Load*.

After completing this chapter, you should be able to:

- Create attributes and measures
- Create different types of attribute view
- Use data foundation, star schema(s), and attribute view to create analytical view
- Learn to hide and create calculated attributes

As we learned earlier in *Chapter 2, SAP HANA Data Modeling Approach*, the business scenario can be represented by Modeling the data in the database tables. It requires that we replicate the relationships and the values by extracting the right data and related entities. We create views for this purpose and this view in HANA is called information model.

To create these information models, we use combination of attribute and measures.

- **Attribute**: Descriptive data, for example, Employee name, Employee ID, and Department
- **Measure**: Quantifiable data, for example, Salary and Bonus

Attributes could be of the following types:

- **Simple attribute**: Non measureable element that comes from the data foundation. (Data foundation represents the tables, used for defining the fact table and the related tables of the view). For example, `Employee_ID` and `Employee_Name`.
- **Calculated attribute**: Derived from one or more existing attributes or constants. For example, assigning a constant value to an attribute that can be used for arithmetic calculations.
- **Local attribute**: We use it in an analytic view and it allows us to customize the behavior of an attribute for only that view.

Similarly, measures could be differentiated into the following types:

- **Simple measures**: These are measurable elements that come from the data foundation; for example: Profit
- **Calculated measures**: These are based on a combination of data from OLAP cubes, arithmetic operators, constants, and functions
- **Restricted measures**: They are used to filter the value based on the user-defined rule for the attribute view
- **Counters**: They are used to add new measure to the calculation view definition to count the recurrence of an attribute

There are three types of information views in SAP HANA:

- **Attribute view**: This view is like dimension, built on one more tables using joins
- **Analytic view**: Star schema or fact table with dimensions, calculation, and restricted measures
- **Calculation view**: This view performs complex calculations which are not possible by the other two

If you want to compare (with SAP BI system), these views are similar to:

SAP HANA	SAP BI
Attribute view	Dimension
Analytical view	Info cube
Calculation view	Multi provider

These SAP HANA views are nonmaterialized views, that is, there would be no latency when the underlying data changes. We will take the discussion further now and start creating the information models. We start with attribute views.

Before we start creating our views, we need to adjust the preferences.

Steps to adjust preferences

1. Go to the **Window** tab on the SAP HANA Studio:

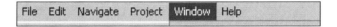

2. Click on **Preferences**:

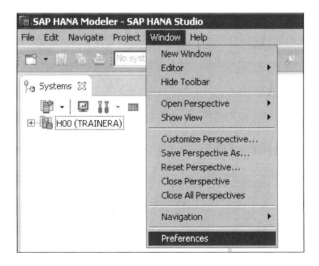

3. Open the **General** folder by clicking the **Open** folder icon:

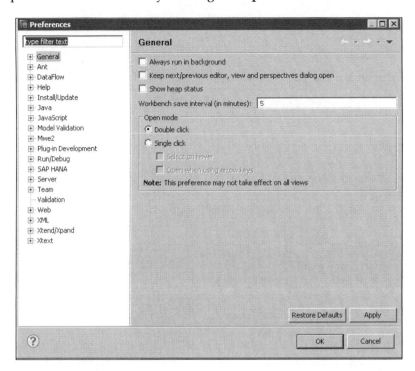

4. Click on **Network Connections:**

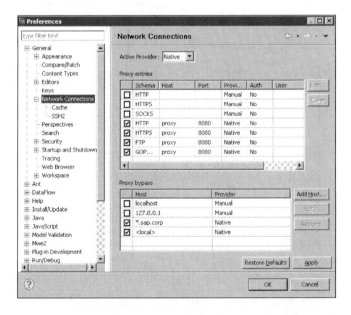

5. Click on **Active Provider** to open a drop-down list:

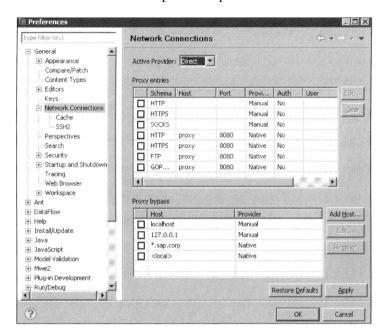

6. Click on **Web Browser**. Select **Use external web browser**:

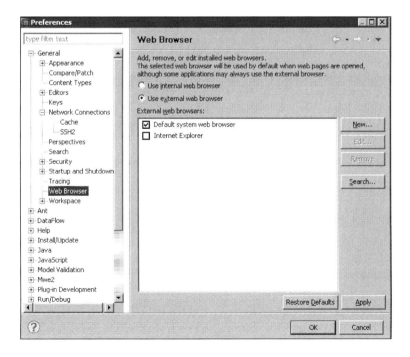

7. Click on **Apply** and then click on the **OK** button. So we have set the required preferences. We already learned how to add system to SAP HANA Studio in *Chapter 2, SAP HANA Data Modeling Approach*. The generic modeling process is: Import source system metadata | provision data | **Create Views** | **Deploy** and **Activate** | consume at end client.

We have already learned about Import source system metadata and data provisioning in the earlier chapters. So we move to the next step – creating views.

Creating attribute views

Attribute views are dimensions, similar to BW characteristics. They are synonymous to master data and can be reused and shared (in analytical and calculation views). Having said that, attribute view is not restricted to master data, but can be created on transactional data as well.

Let's learn how to create it. While creating an attribute view, we have following choice:

*   Using single or multiple tables as data foundation
*   Using existing attribute view

Following are the prerequisites:

*   Tables should exist with data, which we will use for data foundation
*   Package should exist, under which the view would be created

For us, we already have met the prerequisite. In *Chapter 2, SAP HANA Data Modeling Approach*, we learned how to create Package and in *Chapter 3, Different Ways of SAP HANA Data Load*, we saw creation(replication) of a table.

Let's create attribute view step by step, as follows:

1. In the **System** view, right-click on **Package | New | Attribute View**.

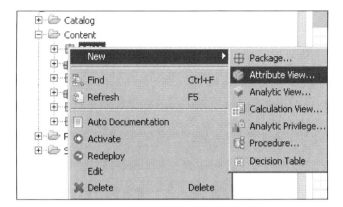

2. Fill the technical name (I follow AT_xx ,as prefix AT helps to identify that it is an attribute view), description, and type of attribute view.

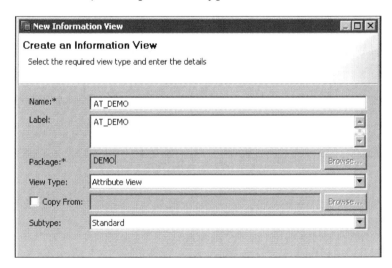

We can create two types of attribute views:

   ° Standard
   ° Time

If we are creating time type attribute view, then we have to mention which type of time data the system has to use (Gregorian/fiscal). We will see it, in more details, later in the chapter.

Attribute view can be classified as follows:

○ **Copy from**: It helps in those cases where you want to use an existing attribute as template. Later, if required, changes can be made.

○ **Derived**: This is kind of a reference type. Here you cannot do modifications to the current one.

On clicking finish, on clicking finish, the next screen appears.

3. Choose the base table – we select the tables on which we are going to build attribute view. For this, we need to click on **Semantics**:

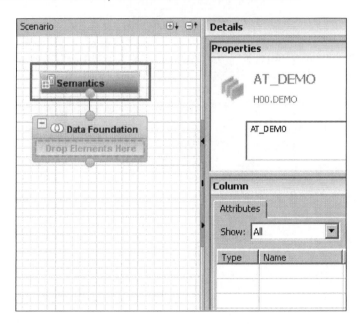

4. We need to add table to data foundation on which we will build our data models. In our case we will use the table(schema) provided by SAP (for the demo purpose). We will be using the tables **SNWD_AD** and **SNWD_BPA**.

So either we can drag and drop the tables from the schema to add it to data foundation.

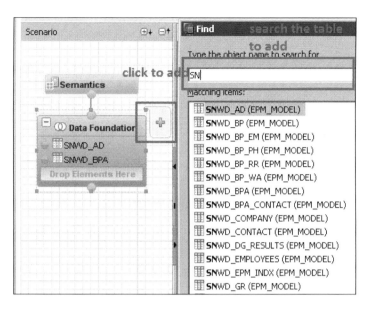

5. Now you can see the tables. We need to join the tables with a common field, in our case **ADDRESS_GUID**.

   You can drag and create the join, or right-click on the field to be joined.

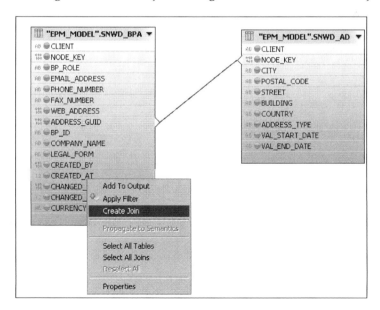

When you click on **Create Join**, you get the following screen to fill in the details:

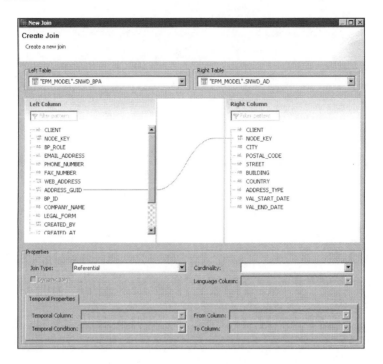

Then choose the fields to be joined and the join type:

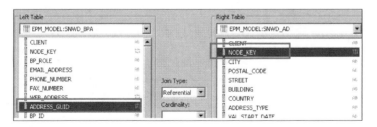

Following are the different types of joins available in SAP HANA, as discussed in *Chapter 1, Kickoff – Before We Start*:

- Referential
- Inner
- Left outer
- Right outer
- Text join and more

In the following screen, Mark the fields that you want as output column

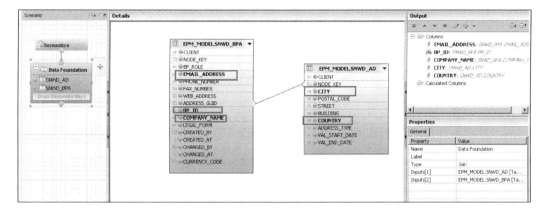

To add to the output column, click on the dot that you see next to the column name. The grey dot will turn into orange when the column is added to output. Click on **Finish**.

Defining attribute and key attribute

Click on **Semantics** | Right-click on **Attribute** | Add as attribute.

When we click on **Semantics**, a pop up appears, where we can see all the columns:

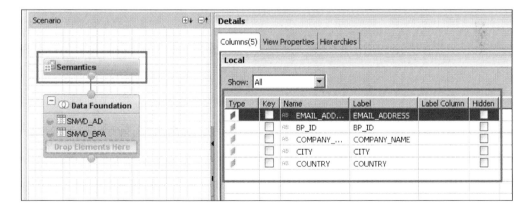

We will make **BP_ID** as key attribute:

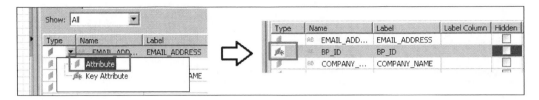

Key attributes are used as the keys when we join this attribute with another Attribute or analytic view.

Right-click any attribute | Add as **Key Attribute**.

In our case, we have taken **BP_ID** as key attribute, and company, city, e-mail address, and country as attribute.

Creating hierarchies is optional while creating attribute views. In SAP HANA, we can create two types of hierarchies:

- **Level based**: This is one to one mapping (one attribute one hierarchy)
- **Parent-child**: This is one to many (one attribute can have multiple hierarchy levels)

We will discuss hierarchy separately in the coming chapters. Save the attribute view and then activate it. Only the activated views will be available for the reporting clients and for data preview as well.

We can identify the difference between the saved and the activated views with the rhombus symbol. Only the saved views will have the rhombus symbol.

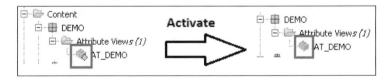

Validation and activation can be done from the system view or from the top bar (right-side of the screen):

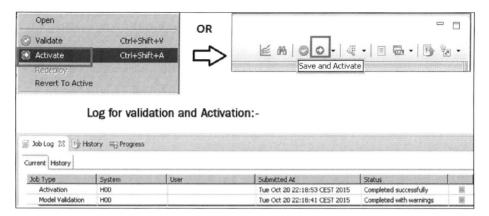

Now we can go to data preview to see the following data in the view.

- Raw data
- Distinct values
- Values

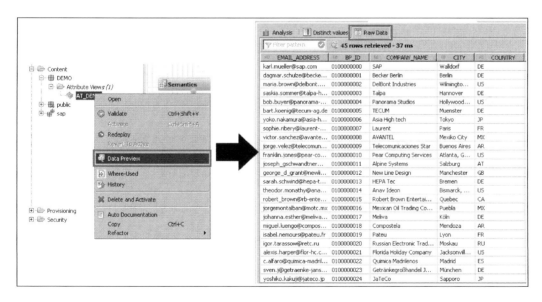

As an assignment, the readers can create two more attribute views, which we will use while creating analytical view in the coming section.

You can create attribute view, you can use following details for creating it.

Name : AT_DEMO2 .

Data Foundation : SNWD_BP, SNWD_BP_EM, SNWD_BP_PH, SNWD_CONTACT.

Name : AT_DEMO2_PRODUCT_MASTER .

Data Foundation : SNWD_PD . "

There is a special type of attribute view called time attribute view. We saw the option previously while choosing the attribute view type during creating it. Let's learn how to create it as well.

Creating time attribute views

The prerequisite are as follows:

- Replicate the standard table into SAP HANA, that is T005T, T005U, T009, and T009B. We need to ask the basis team to do it for us.
- Configure the **Generate Time Data** function. We will do it ourselves, as described next.

Steps involved in creating a time attribute view are:

1. Go to the **Modeler** perspective | **Generate Time data** or from the **Quick Launch**.

2. Fill the details of **Generate Time Data** as shown in the following screen:

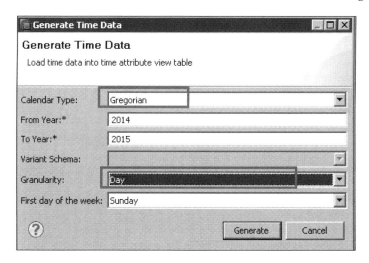

Here I am creating it for year 2014-2015. You can choose the year range for which you want to create the view, and choose the granularity as well accordingly.

3. Go to the **System** view and catalog, and see in schema **_SYS_BI** | table **M_TIME_DIMENSION**.

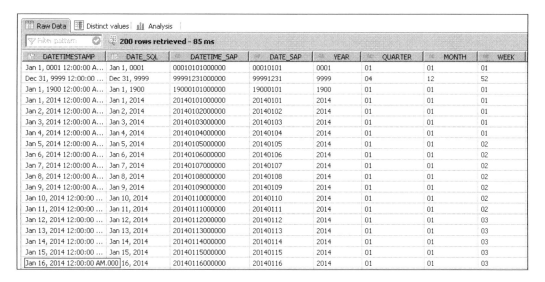

4. Now create a time attribute view with the following details:

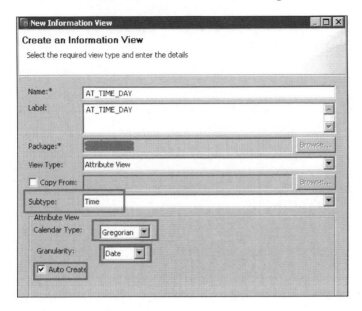

Fill the preceding form with the following details:

- In the **Subtype** field, select **Time** from the drop-down menu
- In the **Calendar Type** field, select **Gregorian** from the drop-down menu
- For the **Granularity** field, select **Date**
- Check on **Auto Create**

After filling the preceding details, click on **Finish**.

5. Now we can add the dimensions table with the generated attributes. We can remove any attribute fields that are not needed.

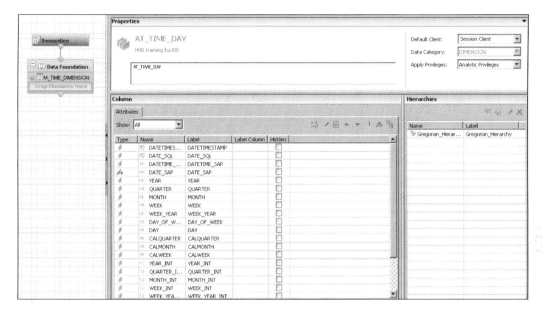

6. **Save** and **Activate** the view. Preview to validate the data, if required.

This time attribute view can be used in another attribute view or in any other analytical view.

As an assignment, the readers can try creating a derived attribute view. A derived attribute view is a linked copy that allows you to use two attribute views with exactly the same definition in the same analytic or calculation view.

Creating analytical views

Analytical views are star schema/fact tables with dimensions, calculation, or restricted measures. Analytic views can contain two types of columns: attributes and measures. As discussed previously, measures are simple, calculated, or restricted. If analytic views are used in the SQL statements, then the measures have to be aggregated. For example, using the SQL functions SUM(<column name>), MIN(<column name>), or MAX(<column name>). Normal columns can be handled as regular attributes and do not need to be aggregated.

Analytical views can be:

- Simple analytical view using database tables
- Enhanced analytical view with attribute view (star schema)

Steps to create analytical view are as follows:

1. Go to **Quick Launch** and click on **Analytical View,** or in the system view, right-click on your package | **New** | **Analytic View**:

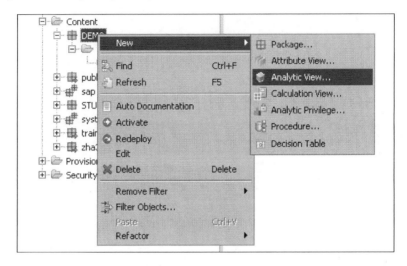

Fill the details as asked in the following screenshot:

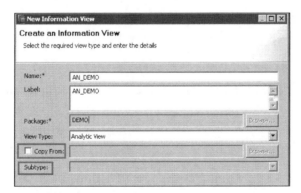

Provide the technical name. Also select whether you are going to create a new analytical view or copy from some other analytic view:

- ° New analytical view
- ° Copy from some other analytic view.

2. You now get to the next screen, where you need to select the base table for your analytic view from the desired schema. As in attribute view, we will use the standard demo schema EPM models provided by SAP, creating an analytical view for the purchase order using table **SNWD_PO** and **SNWD_PO_I**.

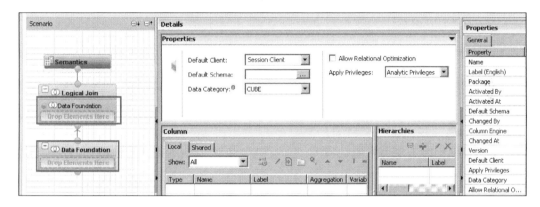

3. Select **Table** and click on **Add** to move the table to the right-side. We can select multiple tables using the control key.

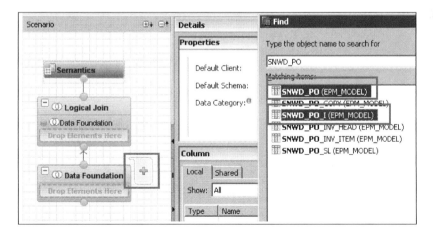

We can select measures only from one table; measures from multiple tables are not possible in analytic view.

1. Join:

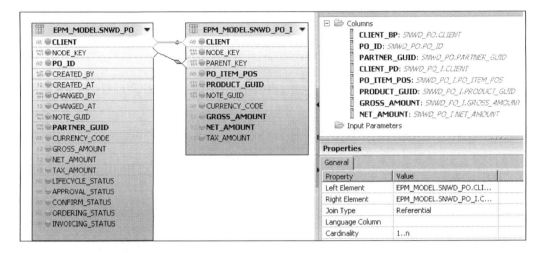

2. To add fields as output columns, use the same method that was used for attribute view:

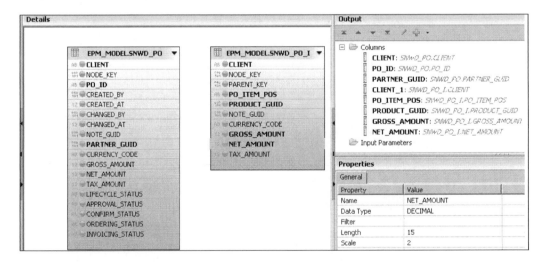

3. Rename the output columns in analytic view:

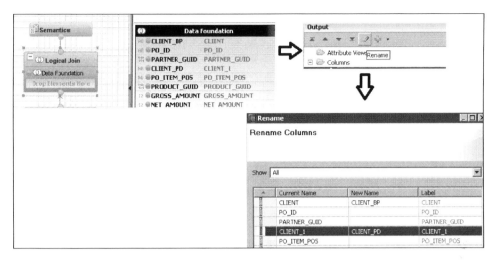

4. Add attribute views from your package. Trust you had created and activated the following attribute view, as an assignment:

    AT_DEMO2: tables used in foundation – SNWD_BP, SNWD_BP_EM, SNWD_BP_PH, SNWD_CONTACT AT_DEMO2_PRODUCT_MASTER: tables used in foundation – SNWD_PD.

5. So now we have table SNWD_PO and SNWD_PO_I data foundation and two Attribute views AT_DEMO1 and AT_DEMO2_PRODUCT_MASTER in the logical join as base for analytical view.

    We will consider **Data Foundation** as the left table and the attribute views as the right tables.

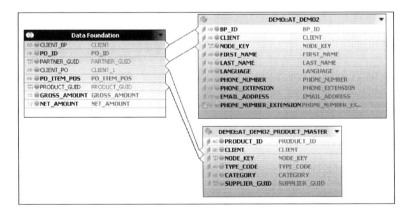

6. We will join the fields, as shown in the preceding diagram. We still go with Referential Join type with `N..1` cardinality:

Data foundation	Attribute view
`CLIENT_PD`	`CLIENT (product master)`
`PRODUCT_GUID`	`NODE_KEY(Product master)`
`PRODUCT_GUID`	`NODE_KEY(Demo1)`
`CLIENT_BP`	`CLIENT(Demo1)`

7. To define the attributes and measures, go to the **Semantics** node:

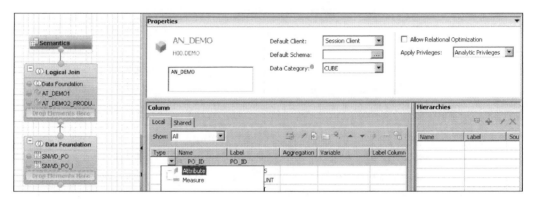

Mark `GROSS_AMOUNT` and `NET_AMOUNT` as measures and all the other columns as attributes:.

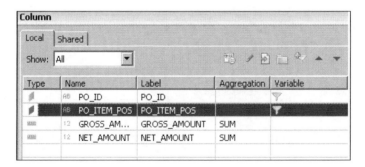

8. **Save** and **Activate** the analytic view. While validating, before activation we get the following pop-up:

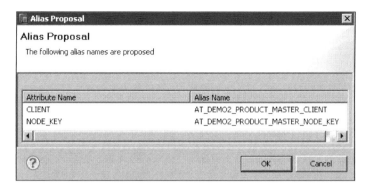

The **CLIENT** and **NODE_KEY** columns exist in both the attributes. Views and the system cannot distinguish between these entities.

So we will accept the proposal and rename the output columns of the attribute view. Now when we activate, it works fine. Preview the data and validate the content.

Creating other elements

Let's learn to create other related elements, which can be used in conjunction with attribute view and analytical view.

Calculated attribute

The following are the steps to create a calculated attribute:

1. Open any of the attribute views created previously.

2. Click on **Data foundation**. In the output pane of the attribute view created previously, right-click **Calculated Attributes**.

3. From the context menu, choose **New.** Give name and description of the calculated attribute that you want to create.

4. Choose the **Key** tab page.

5. Select the data type for the calculated attribute and fill the length and scale.

6. Define the attribute using the required attributes, operator, and function.

7. Drag and drop the required function onto the **Expression Editor**.

8. Click **Add**.

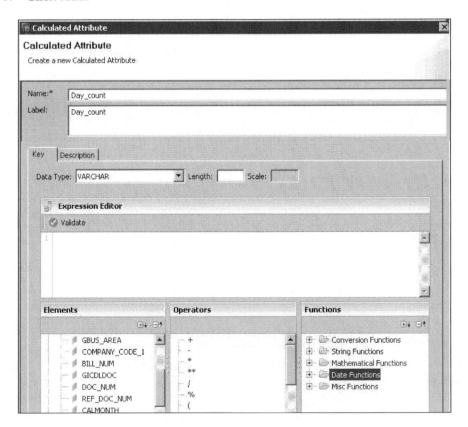

Here we have used **Date Functions**; as per our requirement, we can explore other options as well. We can validate the syntax just by clicking on validate syntax, as shown in the following screenshot:

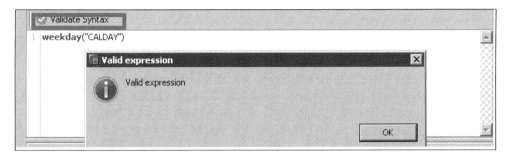

Calculated measures

The steps for creating calculated measures are more or less similar to the steps explained in the preceding example:

1. In the output pane, right-click **Calculated Measures**. From the context menu, choose **New**.

2. Provide the details for the calculated measure.

3. Select the required **Aggregation Type**.

4. If you want to hide the measure while previewing the data, select **Hidden**.

5. Select the required data type for the calculated measure.

6. Define the measure by selecting the required measures, operator, and function.

Calculated columns

Calculated columns are similar to calculated measures in behavior, as you can use existing columns in your formulas in both the cases. If you want to create new columns, which are calculated at runtime, from the existing columns, functions and input parameters and constants.

An example may be that you have a column containing the customers' first and last names. However, you want to have separate columns for the first and the last names. By creating two calculated columns, you can achieve this using string manipulation.

The calculation could be an arithmetic or a character manipulation.

It also supports nonmeasure attributes as part of the calculation. Nesting of calculated column is possible.

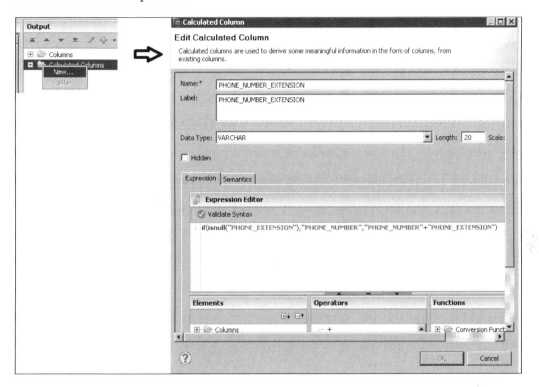

Creating variables

At runtime, you can provide different values to the variables to view the corresponding sets of attribute data. You provide values to the variables either by entering the values manually, or by selecting them from the value help dialog.

The types of supported variables are:

- **Single value**: Use this to filter and view the data based on a single attribute value
- **Interval**: Use this to filter and view a specific set of data
- **Range**: Use this to filter and view the data based on the conditions that involve operators such as `"="`(equal to), `">"` (greater than), and so on

Each type of variable can be either mandatory or nonmandatory. For a mandatory variable, you need to provide a value at runtime. However, for a nonmandatory variable, if you have not specified a value at runtime, you view unfiltered data.

The following are the steps to create a variable:

1. In the **Output** pane, right-click the **Variables** node.

2. From the context menu, choose **New** and provide the following details:

   Similar to other elements: Enter a **Name** | **Description** | required attribute (drop-down list) | required **Selection Type** | **OK**.

At runtime, the value for the variable is fetched from the selected attribute's data.

Self-study questions

1. Create all the views that we did not show previously (for example, derived time, attribute view).

2. Let's say you create an analytical view and you want a particular attribute to behave differently than it does in the attribute view to which it belongs; how can this be achieved?

3. What is refactoring object ? Can analytical views be refactored?

Summary

In this chapter ,we defined attributes and measures, their types, and learned how to create them. To have better accessibility and ease in the view creation ,we learned and adjusted the preferences. After setting the preferences ,we took a closer look at attribute view and created standard and time attribute views. Once attribute view was created, we used the same, along with the standard tables, to create analytical view. We also learned about other elements which can be used with attribute view and analytical view, such as calculated columns, measures, and variables, and also learned how they can be created.

In the next chapter, we will continue with SAP HANA artifacts and learn about analytical privileges and calculation view. We will also learn about various other components involved during creation of these artifacts.

5
Creating SAP HANA Artifacts – Analytical Privileges and Calculation Views

In the previous chapter, we learned how to create information models—attribute view and analytical view. We also walked through various other components involved during the creation of these artifacts. We will continue with the creation of other SAP HANA information models in this chapter namely—calculation view and analytical view. We will also explore how to create and use filters and input variables.

After completing this chapter, you should be able to:

- Create restricted measures and restricted columns
- Create filters, variables and input parameters (This is covered in this chapter in more detail)
- Create calculation view—graphical
- Create and use analytical privileges

In *Chapter 4, Creating SAP HANA Artifacts Attribute Views and Analytical Views*, under other elements, we learned how to create calculated measures and calculated columns. Let's learn some more basic elements before we move on to create calculation view and analytical privileges.

Creating a restricted measure and a calculated measure

First of all, we will create a new analytical view (I hope you learned it well in the last chapter to do it yourself now). We will use two tables as the base table — `sales` and `product` (the table definition and sample data can be downloaded from Packt Publishing website). Re-verify that the structure of the table is as follows:

The following screenshot shows the `Sales` table:

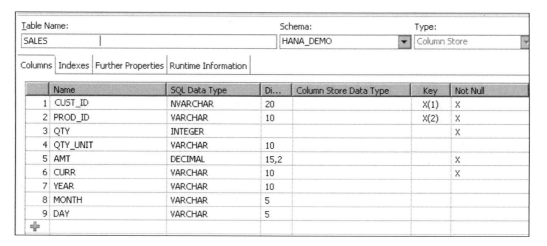

The following screenshot shows the `Product` table:

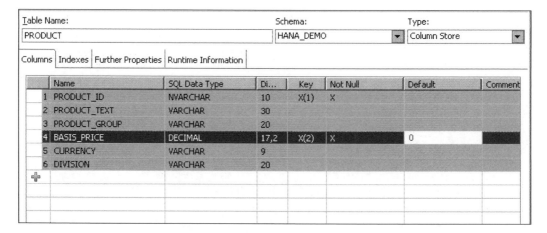

Steps to create restricted measure and calculated measure:

1. Our analytical view should look like this with joins:

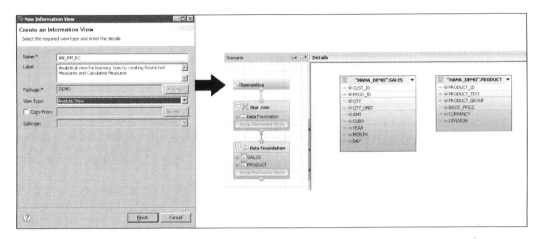

2. The join type is referential, with a cardinality of 1..N (PRODUCT to SALES table). Join the tables as shown in the following screenshot:

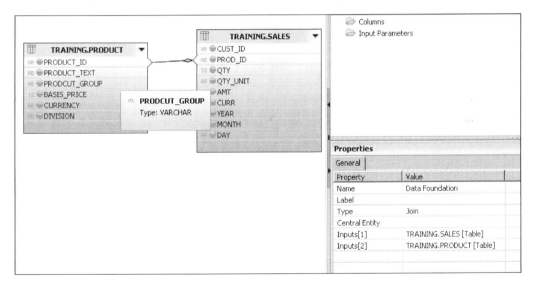

3. Add to **Output | SALES.CURR** and **PRODUCT.PRODUCT_TEXT**.

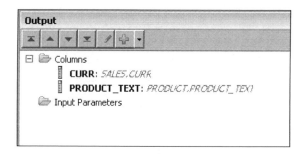

4. In the **Semantics** node, set the type for both columns to attribute. Select the hidden flag for the **PRODUCT_TEXT** attribute.

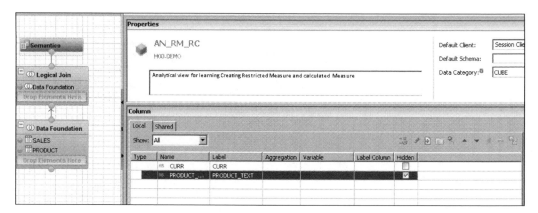

5. In the **Semantic** node, define the type for **AMT** as **Measure**:

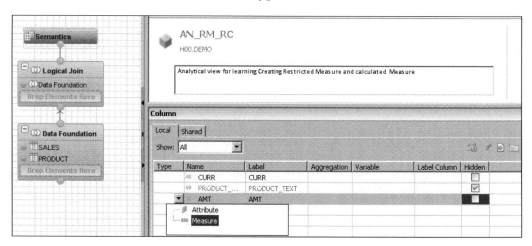

6. Rename the measure (Rename **AMT** | `Total_sales`) in the logical join:

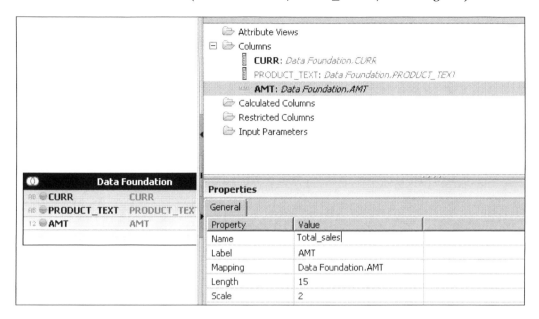

7. Now let's learn how to create a restricted column, and we will add the restricted columns to this example as well. In the **Output** view of the analytical view, go to **Logical Join** (node), right-click on the **Restricted Column** folder and select new from the context menu:

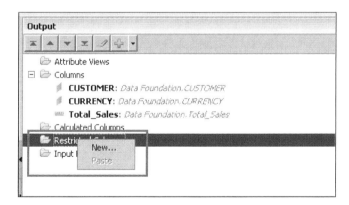

8. Fill in the details as show in the following screenshot, we are selecting the **Equal** operator and assigning values to it:

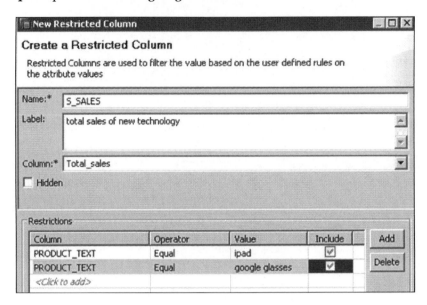

9. Once created, you can see it in the output column of the logical join node.

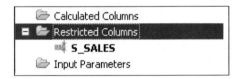

10. Save and activate the analytical view.

You can see the data preview, and you will now see that the simple measure and restricted columns that you just created are available here.

Let's now add a calculation column:

1. We will use the same analytical view that we created previously.

2. In the **Logical Join** node, right-click on **Calculated Column** and choose **New Calculated Column...** from the context menu:

3. Fill the required values, as shown in the following screenshot. Set the **S_SALES/Total Sales, Data Type** expression as **DECIMAL** and **Column Type** as **MEASURE**.

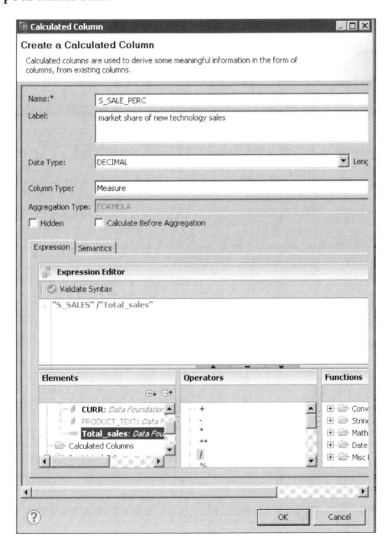

4. Similarly, you can create an N number of calculated columns on various expression logics.

5. Once you are done, you can save the analytic view and activate it.

6. You can do the data preview again. Now you will notice that in addition to the previously created restricted columns, you have some calculated columns as well.

Creating filters

The first question that comes to our mind is why do we need filters? As discussed in *Chapter 2, SAP HANA Data Modeling Approach, Modeling Principles* section — consideration to make in *Chapter 1, Kickoff – Before We Start*: The idea is to filter the data at the lowest layer and only bring the data that is actually required by the query. (Quoting it from *Chapter 1, Kickoff – Before We Start*).That is, we should try to reduce data transfer between the engines. This can be achieved using the following steps:

1. Creating client dependent views: The data is automatically filtered to one client.

2. Using domain fix values: This can be used for several fields.

3. Creating filters: This is defined during design time.

4. Creating and using the WHERE clauses in queries: This is defined at the runtime of the SQL query.

Using the preceding steps not only ensures that we minimize data transfer between the engines, but also helps to reduce the larger result sets between the HANA database and the client/application. The general recommendations are always the following:

*   The data, if and wherever possible, should be aggregated and filtered to a manageable size before it leaves the data layer.

*   When deciding the records that should be reported upon, the best practice approach is to think at the **set level** and not at the **record level**. By set level, I mean aggregating the data by a certain criteria such as year/month, plant, sales region, and so on. Thereby minimizing the amount of data passed between views.

Steps for creating a filter

1. Create an attribute view (**AT_REGION_Filter**) to show data across different clients/Mandet.

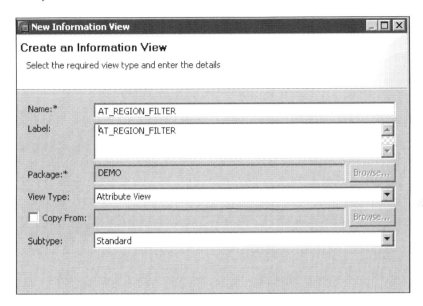

2. Here the steps to create the attribute view are not shown, as we have already learned them. Make sure that you have added the REGION_EXT table to **Data Foundation**. Create it the same way we created a table in *Chapter 1, Kickoff – Before We Start*. It will have following fields:

REGION_ID	REGION_NAME	SUB_AREA	MANDT
100	Europe	Germany	100
200	Asia	Japan	200
300	US	Northfields	300

It is a part of the sample table/data available on our website. Download the table from there.

3. Add all these columns to the output of **Data Foundation**: REGION_ID, REGION_NAME, SUB-AREA, and MANDET.

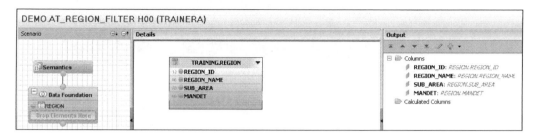

4. Add to **Output** from the context menu.

5. Go to **Semantics** and double-click it/select it. On Right of your screen you see the following screen. Go to **Default Client** and change it from session to **Cross Client**.

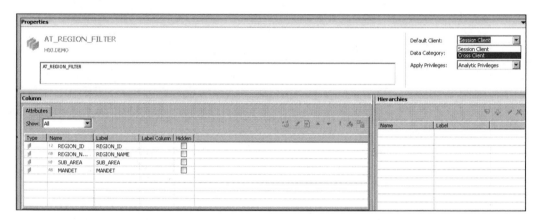

6. Define REGION_NAME as **Key Attribute** in the **Semantic** node of the view.

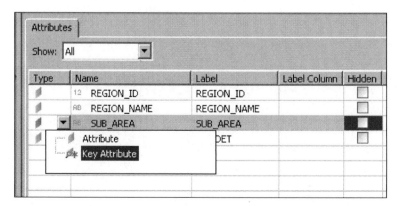

7. Save and activate the view.

8. In **Data Preview,** go to **Raw Data | Distinct Values**, select **REGION_NAME,** and observe and mark the result (you should write this down somewhere).

   Now let's change our **AT_REGION_Filter** attribute view and see what happens if we do step 8 again.

9. Open the attribute view again in **AT_REGION_Filter**.

10. Now we will change **Default Client** from **Cross Client** to **Session Client**.

11. Save and activate the view.

12. In **Data Preview**, choose **Raw Data** and see the result.

13. Then go to **Distinct Values**, select **REGION_NAME,** and observe and mark the result (you should write this down somewhere).

Compare the results before and after the change of the default client. Now let's learn how to create a constraint filter. Our intention here is to show only one of the four columns from the **REGION_EXT** table. Let's say that we only want to show **SUB_AREA**. For this, we will follow these steps:

1. We will use the same attribute view that was previously created in **AT_REGION_Filter**.

2. Reset **Default Client** to **Cross Client** again.

3. Go to **Data Foundation,** right-click on **Apply Filters**, and place the filter as shown in the following screenshot:

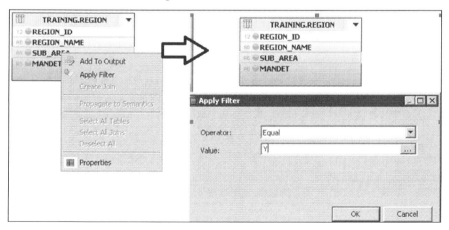

4. **Save** and **Activate** the attribute view.

5. Now again check the **Distinct Values** tab of **Data Preview** and select **SUB_AREA**.

6. The result must be different from what we saw in the previous two cases.

Creating input parameters and variables

Input parameters are used for formulas and can have any value a reporting user might enter. In SQL, it is passed using a placeholder. Variables are used for filtering and always applied to an attribute/s.

The following are the steps to create input parameters and variables:

1. Create an analytical view using the CUSTOMER and SALES tables.

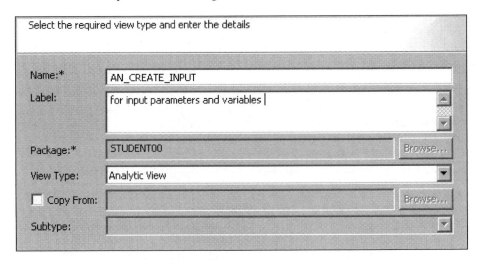

2. Our analytical view should look like this:

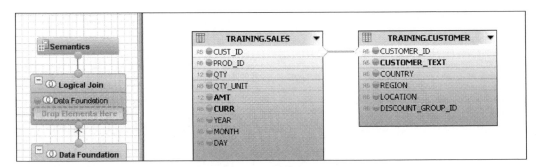

3. The cardinality, output columns, and measures should match as follows:

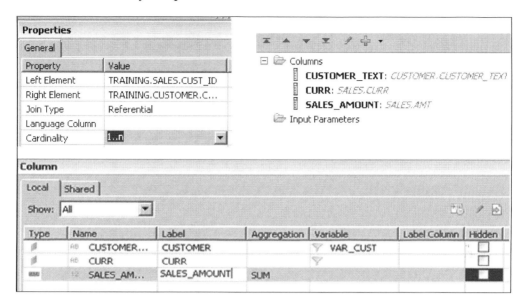

4. Go to the **Semantic** node and click on the + notation.

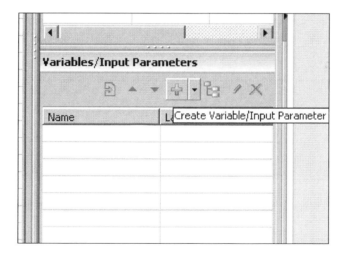

5. Provide the details and mark the attribute on which you want to create the variable.

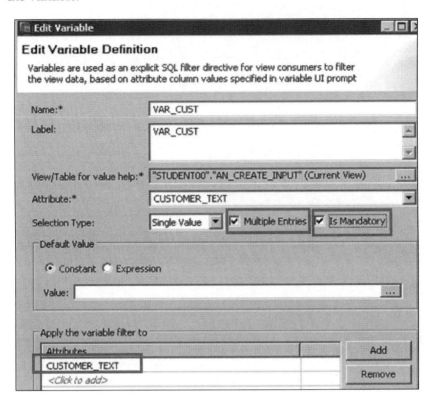

6. Then save and activate the analytical view.

7. We can do the data preview. When you click on **Data Preview**, a popup appears as shown in the following screenshot:

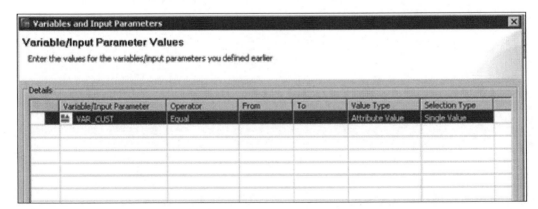

8. We must click on **From** (and choose a value) and **To** (again, choose a value).
9. Click on **OK** and again on **OK**. Then, click on the **Raw Data** tab.
10. You can see the data for the values of the variables that you choose from.

As a self assignment, you can play around with various other options such as input parameters and more calculated columns.

So now we are ready with the basics, and we can proceed to the calculation view creation.

Creating calculation views

Calculation views are composite views that are used to calculate complex tabular results using either explicit SQL script code or a data flow graph that is visually created in the SAP HANA Studio. It can consume other analytical/attribute/calculation views and tables. It can perform complex calculations that are not possible with other views.

The calculation views are of the following types:

*   Graphical calculation views are created using the graphical editor
*   Scripted calculation views are created using the SQL editor

Complex calculations, which are not possible through the graphical approach, can be created using SQLscript. Calculation views can be used in the same way as analytic views.

In contrast to analytic views, it is possible to join several fact tables in a calculation view where measures are selected from the different fact tables.

We will use the standard EPM data that is given as IDES data in SAP HANA. Our calculation view would be for sales orders from two different source systems (using the standard SAP EPM data provided). To create a graphical calculation view, the following are the steps:

1. In the **System** view, go to **Content** node, right-click on the package, and choose **New | Calculation View...**

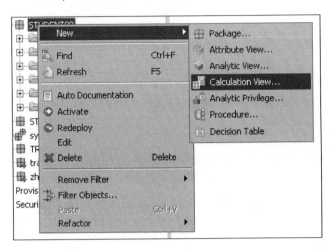

You are asked to filled the following details of the calculation view you want to create.

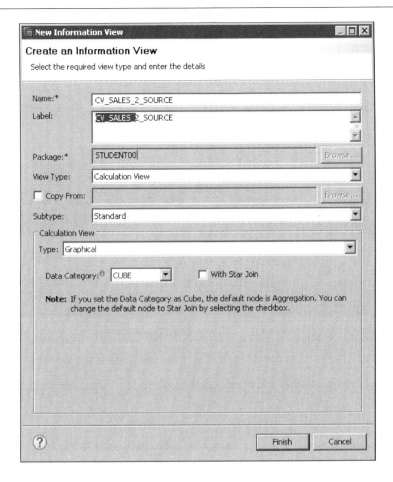

The Data category could be of two types—cube or dimension. The difference is marked as shown in the following screenshots:

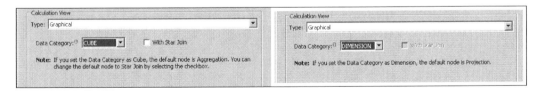

We choose **Cube**:

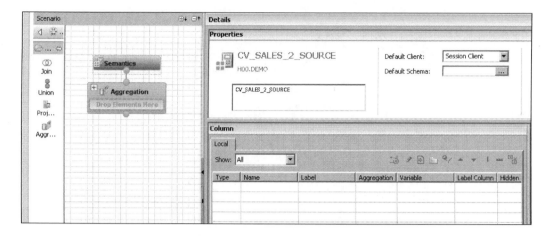

2. Add an **Aggregation** node as shown in the following diagram. Aggregation nodes are used to have a control on how the aggregation is calculated. We can add calculated columns with measures to the node (calculation would be performed after aggregation).

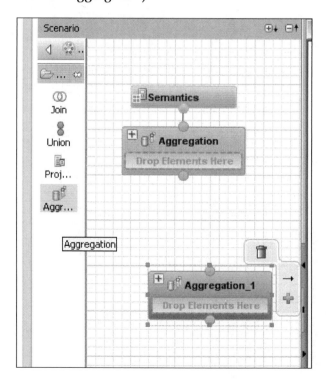

3. Rename the new aggregation node as **SAP_ERP**.

4. Right-click the new **Aggregation Node**, select **Rename** from the context menu, and enter **SAP_ERP**. Then, click **OK**.

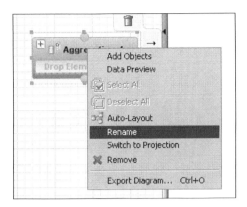

5. Assign the **EPM_MODEL.SNWD_SO** table to the aggregation node. From the catalog node, drag the **EPM_MODEL.SNWD_SO** table to the aggregation node.

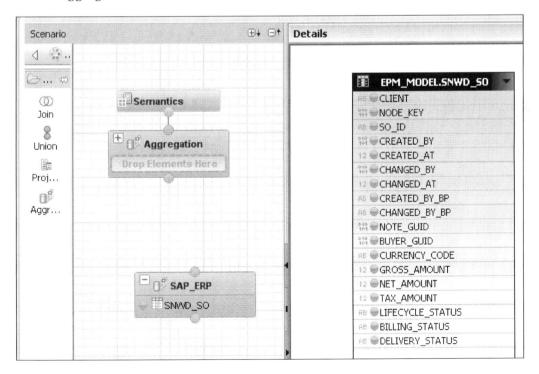

6. Select the **SAP_ERP** aggregation node and add the following columns to output: **CLIENT, CURRENCY_CODE**.

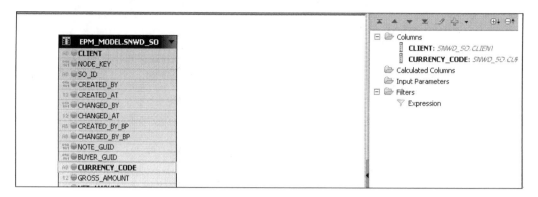

7. Select the **SAP_ERP** aggregation node, right-click on the preceding columns individually in the details panel, and select **Add to Output** from the context menu.

Add the following columns as aggregated columns:

   ° **GROSS_AMOUNT**

   ° **NET_AMOUNT**

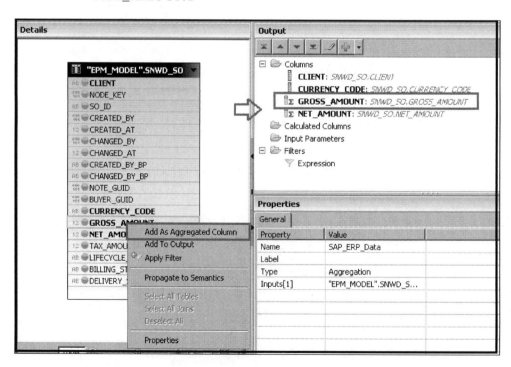

Right-click on the preceding columns individually in the details pane, Selecting **Add as Aggregated Column** from the context menu. Aggregated columns are used for measures. Now let's learn how to add data from a third-party/external source to our calculation view in the following steps:

1. Add another aggregation node; create the new node based on the **DEMO. SALES** table (the one that you used earlier), as shown in the following screenshot:

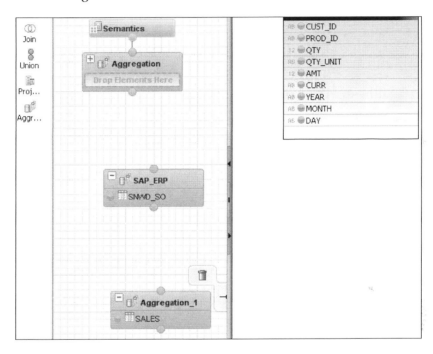

2. Rename this aggregation node as: **3rd_party**. Right-click on the new aggregation node, select **Rename**, enter **3rd_party,** and click on **OK**.

3. Add the **CURRENCY (CURR)** column to the output. Select the **3rd_party** aggregation node and right-click on **Add To Output**.

4. Add the **AMOUNT (AMT)** column as an aggregated column. Right-click on **Selecting Add as Aggregated Column**.

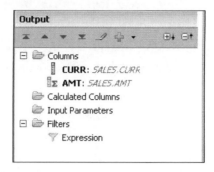

5. We do not have a net amount in **3rd_party**. So in the **3rd_party** aggregation node, add a calculated column using the details shown in the following screenshot:

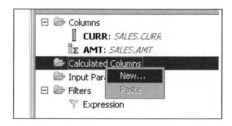

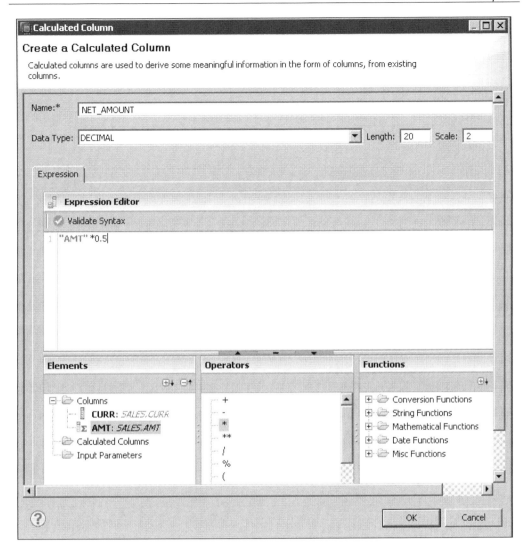

6. Create a second calculated column just for the sole purpose of data type conversion.

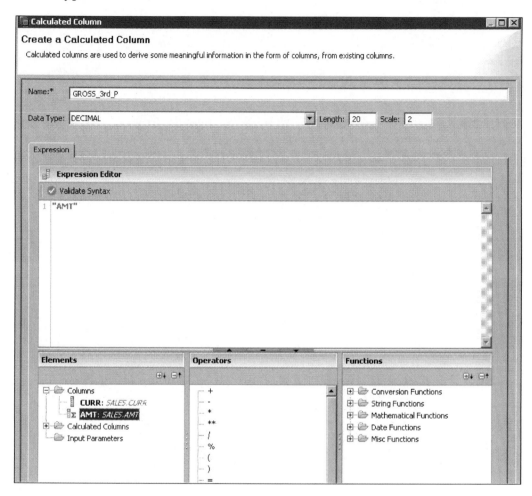

7. Combine the two data sources using a Union node as shown in the following screenshot:

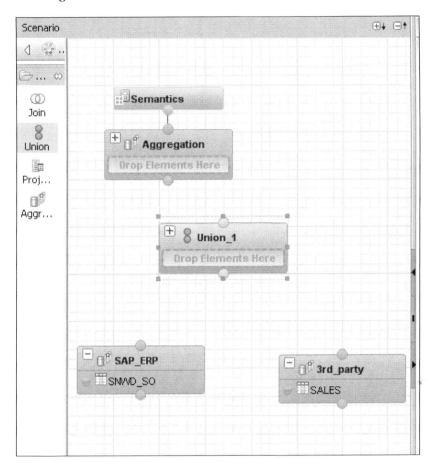

8. Connect the **SAP_ERP** and **3rd_party** aggregation nodes to the **Union** node. We can use the mouse to drag and drop or just right-click and **Add to Target**.

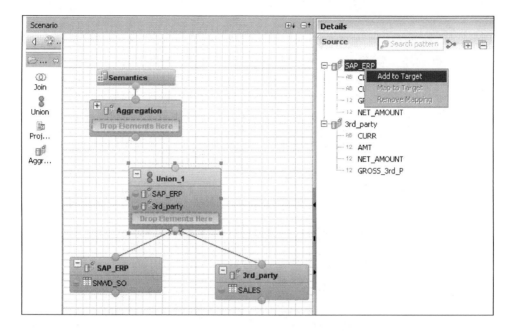

9. In the details of the union node, drag all the columns of the **SAP_ERP** source from **Source** to **Target**.

10. From **3rd_party Source**, drag the following columns to **Target** individually, as shown in the following screenshot:

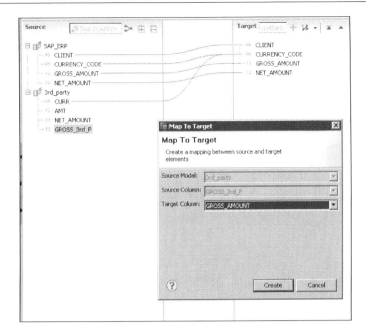

The third-party data does not contain **CLIENT**, which is 800 for the SAP data.

You need to hard code the client with the value 800 for the third-party data.

11. To manage a column mapping, right-click the target column. Select **Manage Mappings** from the context menu, as shown in the following screenshot:

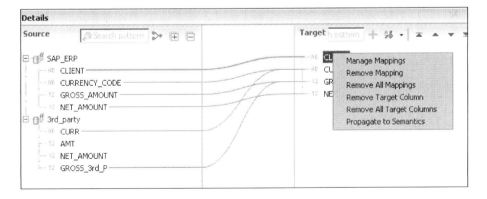

12. Enter **Constant Value** as **800** for **Source Model** as **3rd_party**. Click on **OK**.

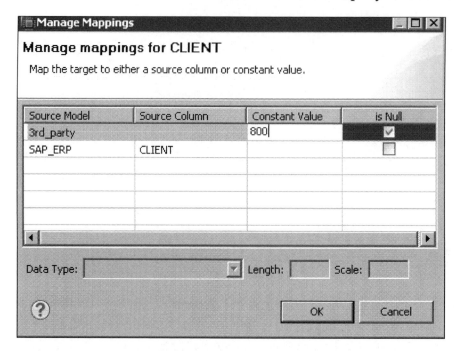

13. In this scenario, connect the union node to the uppermost aggregation node as shown in the following screenshot:

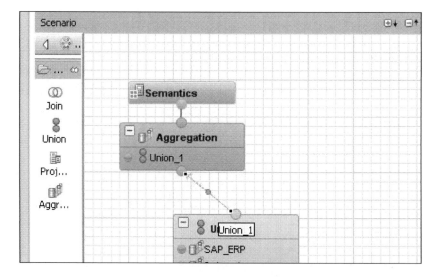

14. In the uppermost aggregation node, add **CLIENT** and **CURRENCY_CODE** to output (nonaggregated columns).

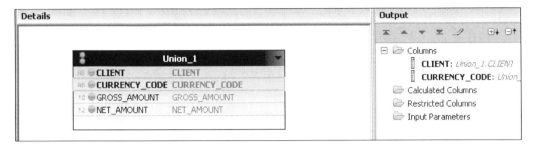

15. Add **GROSS_AMOUNT** and **NET_AMOUNT** as aggregated columns.

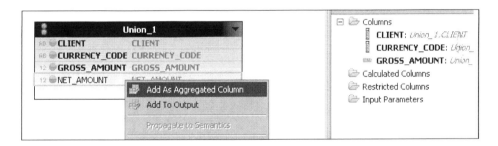

16. **Save** and **Activate**.

17. Perform a data preview of your model and go to the **Raw Data** tab.

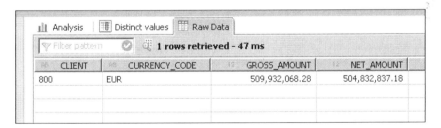

Analytical privileges

Analytical privileges are used to provide fine-grained control of what data a particular user can see for analytic use. They provide the ability to control access to SAP HANA data models.

You can implement row-level security with analytic privileges. You can also restrict access to selected attribute values in a given data container, such as field from attribute view, field from the attribute view used in an analytic view private dimension of the analytic view, attribute field in calculation view, combinations of the above and much more.

To create analytical privileges, perform the following:

1. In the **System** view, got to the **Content** node, right-click on the package, and choose **New | Analytical Privilege**.

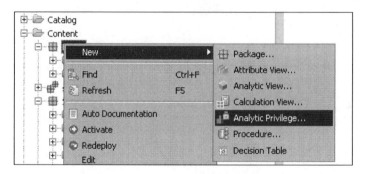

2. Fill in details such as **Name** and **Label**:

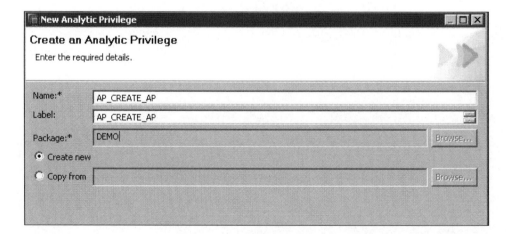

3. Then, we will have to select one of the information models that we want to use for our analytical privileges. I will use the calculation view that we just created:

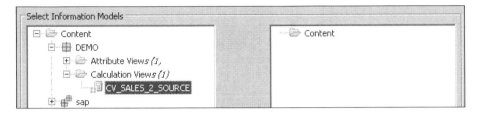

Once you are done with the preceding selection, you will get the following screen:

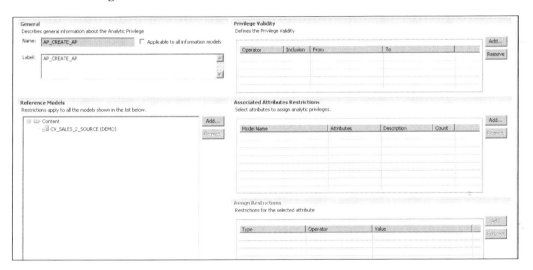

4. Under **Associated Attributes Restriction**, click **Add** | In the **Select Object** window, select **CLIENT** and click **OK**.

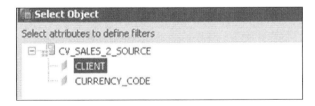

5. Go to **Assign Restrictions**, click **Add**.

6.   Choose **Type** as **Fixed** and **Operator** as **Equal**. In the **Value** column, click and then select **CLIENT** as **800** as shown in the following screenshot:

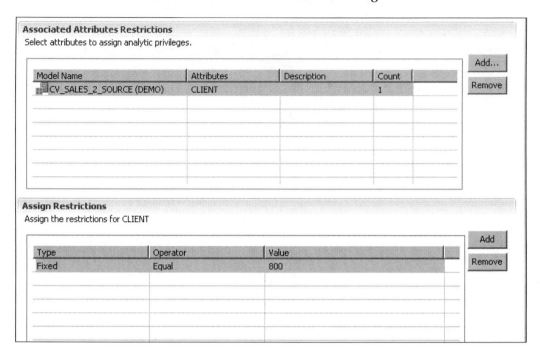

7.   Save and activate the analytic privilege.

8.   To test this, we need to assign it first to a user and remove all their other analytical privileges.

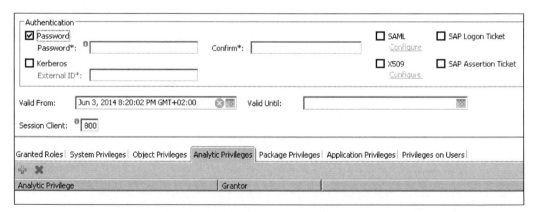

9. Then assign only the privilege that we just created for them.

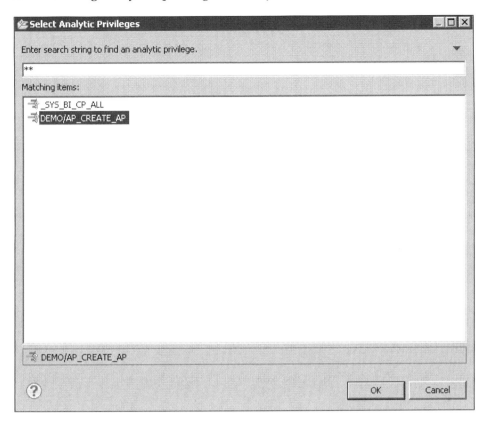

10. Now we should do a data preview with this user, and we should only see client 800 data.

We are not discussing the entire security concept of SAP HANA, as it is beyond the scope of this book and the target audience would be very much different. This brings us to the end of SAP HANA artifacts creation. Hope you have learned how-to perform the steps nicely. My general suggestion would be to think of some small scenarios and re-create the whole thing on your own.

Self-study questions

1. Create an analytic privilege using a procedure as an attribute filter.

2. Create a scripted calculation view.

3. What are counters?

4. If you do not include measures in the calculation view, will it work? How will it behave?

Summary

In this chapter, we progressed towards more complex concepts of information modeling. We learned how to create restricted measures and restricted columns. We went further in to the concepts of filters, variables and input parameters and created our own variables. Once the basic building blocks for calculation view were ready, we learned how to create the calculation view graphically. We also learned about analytical privileges and used them to restrict access to the calculation view that we created.

In the next chapter, we will learn about hierarchies and text search in SAP HANA; how to create and use them in our data models for real-time analytics. We will learn how to make use of hierarchies in business intelligence reporting to display characteristics across aggregated nodes. We will explore the benefits of text search in data mining and extracting useful information out of huge amounts of data.

6
Understanding Text Search and Hierarchies in SAP HANA

Until the previous chapter, we were working on the information model, learning how to create the model, and its prerequisites. We completed the concept with a calculation view and analytical privilege creation. This chapter covers Full Text Search and hierarchies in SAP HANA, and how to create and use them in our data models.

After completing this chapter, you should be able to:

- Create and use Full Text Search
- Create hierarchies — level and parent-child hierarchies

Creating and using Full Text Search

Before we proceed with the creation and use of Full Text Search, let's quickly go through the basic terms associated with it. They are as follows:

- **Text Analysis**: This is the process of analyzing unstructured text, extracting relevant information, and then transforming this information into structure information that can be leveraged in different ways. The scripts provide additional possibilities to analyze strings or large text columns by providing analysis rules for many industries in many languages for SAP HANA.

- **Full Text Search**: This capability of HANA helps to speed up search capabilities within large amounts of text data significantly. The primary function of Full Text Search is to optimize linguistic searches.

- **Fuzzy Search**: This functionality enables us to find strings that match a pattern approximately (rather than exactly). It's a fault-tolerant search, meaning that a query returns records even if the search term contains additional or missing characters, or even spelling mistakes. It is an alternative to a non-fault tolerant SQL statement.

- **The score() function**: When using `contains()` in the `where` clause of a `select` statement, the `score()` function can be used to retrieve the score. This is a numeric value between `0.0` and `1.0`. The score defines the similarity between the user input and the records returned by the search. A score of 0.0 means that there is no similarity. The higher the score, the more similar a record is to the search input.

Some of the applied applications of fuzzy search could be:

- Fault-tolerant check for duplicate records. Its helps to prevent duplication entry in Systems by searching similar entries.

- Fault-tolerant search in text columns — for example, search documents on diode and find all documents that contain the term "triode".

- Fault-tolerant search in structure database content search for rhyming words, for example coffee Krispy biscuit and find toffee crisp biscuits (the standard example given by SAP).

Let's see the use cases for text search:

- Combining structured and unstructured data
  - Medicine and healthcare
  - Patents
  - Brand monitoring and the buying patterns of consumers

- Real-time analytics on a large volume of data
  - Data from social media
  - Finance data
  - Sales optimization
  - Monitoring and production planning

The results of text analysis are stored in a table and therefore, can be leveraged in all the HANA- supported scenarios:

- **Standard Analytics**: Create analytical views and calculation views on top. For example, companies mentioned in news articles over time.

- **Data mining, predictive**: Facilitate use of R language, **Predictive Analysis Library (PAL)** functions for cases like clustering, time series analysis and so on.

- **Search-based applications**: Create a search model and build a search UI with the HANA Info Access (InA) toolkit for HTML5. Text analysis results can be used to navigate and filter search results. For example, People finder, and a search UI UI for internal documents.

The capabilities of HANA Full Text Search and text analysis are as follows:

- Native full text search
- Database text analysis
- The graphical modeling of search models
- Info Access toolkit for HTML5 UIs.

The benefits of full text search:

- Extract unstructured content with no additional cost
- Combine structured and unstructured information for unified information access
- Less data duplication and transfer
- Harness the benefit of InA (Info Access toolkit) for an HTML5 application

The following are the supported data types by fuzzy search:

- Short text
- Text
- VARCHAR
- NVARCHAR
- Date
- Data with full text index.

Enabling the search option

Before we can use the search option in any attribute or analytical view, we will need to enable this functionality in the SAP HANA Studio Preferences as shown in the following screenshot:

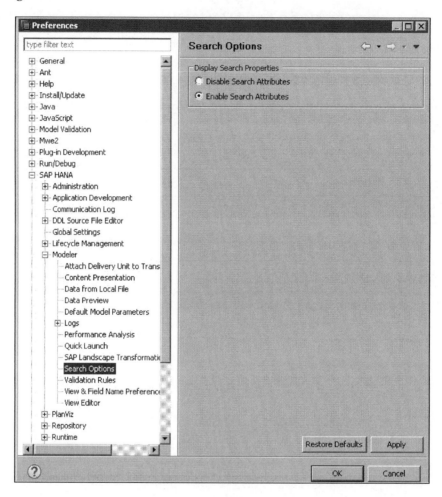

We are well prepared to move ahead with the creation and use of Full Text search. Let's do this step by step as follows:

1. Create the table that we will use to perform the Full Text Search statements:

```
Create Schema <DEMO>; // I am creating , it would be already
present from our previous exercises .
SET SCHEMA DEMO; // Set the schema name
Create a Column Table including FUZZY SEARCH indexed columns.
DROP TABLE DEMO.searchtbl_FUZZY;
```

```
CREATE COLUMN TABLE DEMO.searchtbl_FUZZY (
   CUST_NAME TEXT FUZZY SEARCH INDEX ON,
   CUST_COUNTY TEXT FUZZY SEARCH INDEX ON,
   CUST_DEPT TEXT FUZZY SEARCH INDEX ON,
   );
```

2. Prepare the fuzzy search logic (SQL logic):

Search for customers in the countries that contain the `'MAIN'` word:

```
SELECT score() AS score, *
FROM searchtbl_FUZZY
WHERE CONTAINS(cust_county, 'MAIN');
```

Search for customers in the countries that contain the `'MAIN'` word but with Fuzzy parameter 0.4)

```
SELECT score() AS score, *
FROM searchtbl_FUZZY
WHERE CONTAINS(cust_county, 'West', FUZZY(0.3));
```

Perform a fuzzy search for a customer working in a department that includes the `department` word :

```
SELECT highlighted(cust_dept), score() AS score, *
FROM searchtbl_FUZZY
WHERE CONTAINS(cust_dept, 'Department', FUZZY(0.5));
```

Fuzzy search for all the columns by looking for the `customer` word:

```
SELECT score() AS score, *
FROM searchtbl_FUZZY
WHERE CONTAINS(*, 'Customer', FUZZY(0.5));
```

Creating hierarchies

Hierarchies are created to maintain data in a structured format, such as maintaining customer or employee data based on their roles and splitting the data based on geographies. Hierarchical data is very useful for organizational purposes during decision making.

Two types of hierarchies can be created in SAP HANA:

- The level hierarchy
- Parent-child hierarchy

The hierarchies are initially created in the attribute view and later can be combined in the analytic view or calculation view for consumption in a report as per business requirements. Let's create both types of hierarchies in attribute views.

Creating a level hierarchy

Each level represents a position in the hierarchy. For example, a time dimension might have a hierarchy that represents data at the month, quarter, and year levels. Each level above the base level contains aggregate values for the levels below it.

The following are the steps to create level hierarchy:

1. Create a new attribute view (for your own practice, I would suggest you to create a new one). You can also use an existing one. Use the SNWD_PD EPM sample tables.

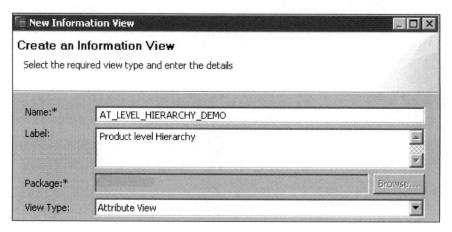

2. In output view, mark the following as output:

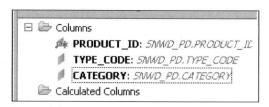

3. In the semantic node of the view, create a new hierarchy as shown in the following screenshot and fill in the details:

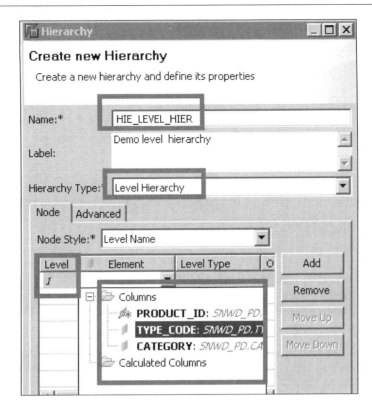

4. Save and activate the view.

5. Now the hierarchy is ready to be used in an analytical view.

   Add a client and node key again as output to your attribute view that you just created, that is AT_LEVEL_HIERARCY_DEMO, as we will use these two fields in our hierarchy

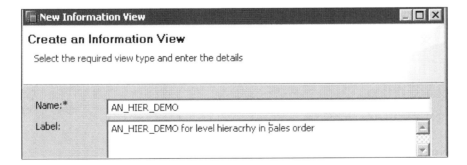

6. Create an analytical view. It should look like the following screenshot.

Add the attribute view created in the preceding step and the SNWD_SO_I table to the data foundation:

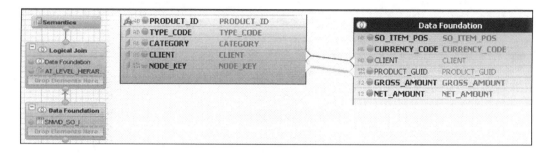

7. Join client to client and product guide to node key:

1. Save and activate.

2. Go to MS Excel | **All Programs** | **Microsoft Office** | **Microsoft Excel 2010** then go to **Data** tab | **From Other Sources** | **From Data Connection Wizard**.

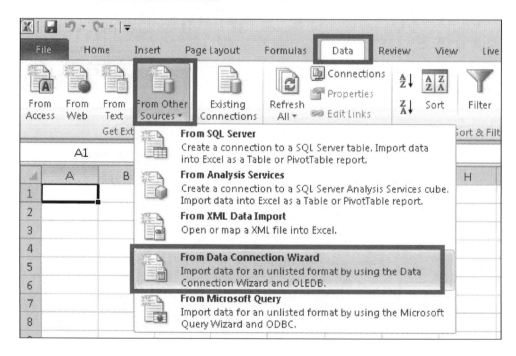

3. You will get a new popup for **Data Connection Wizard** | **Other/Advanced** | **SAP HANA MDX Provider**:

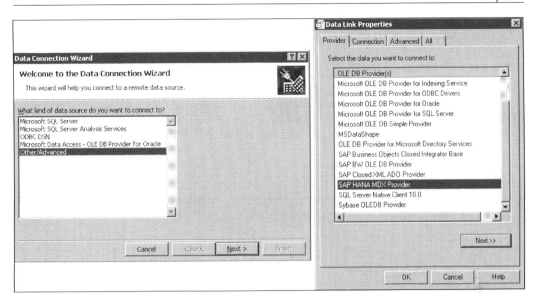

4. You will be asked to provide the connection details, fill in the details, and test the connection (these are the same details that you used while adding the system to SAP HANA Studio).

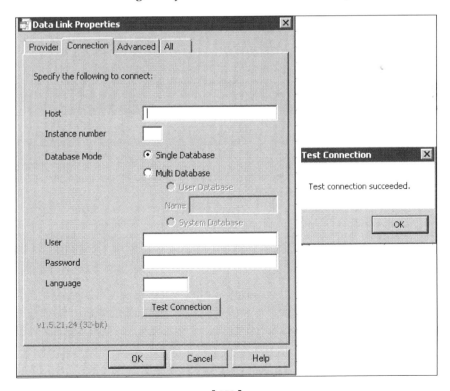

5. **Data Connection Wizard** will now ask you to choose the analytical view (choose the one that you just created in the preceding step):

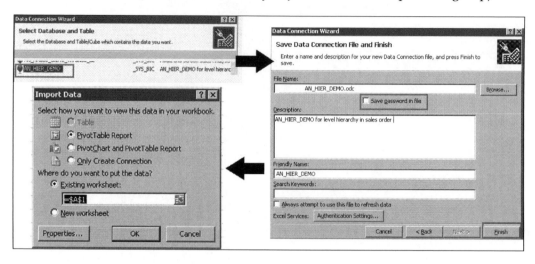

6. The preceding steps will take you to an excel sheet and you will see data as per the choices that you chose in the Pivot table field list:

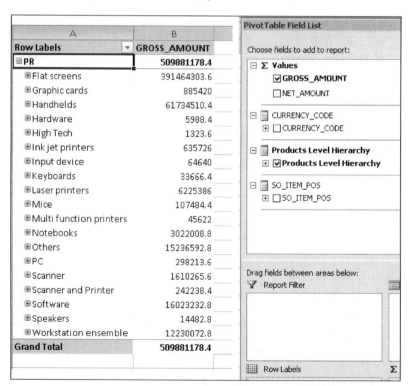

Creating a parent-child hierarchy

The parent-child hierarchy is a simple, two-level hierarchy where the child element has an attribute containing the parent element. These two columns define the hierarchical relationships among the members of the dimension. The first column, called the member key column, identifies each dimension member. The other column, called the parent column, identifies the parent of each dimension member. The parent attribute determines the name of each level in the parent-child hierarchy and determines whether the data for parent members should be displayed.

Let's create a parent-child hierarchy using the following steps:

1. Create an attribute view.

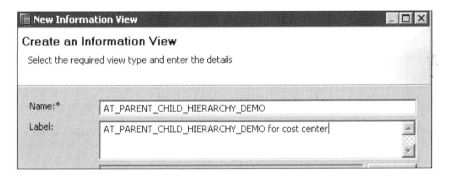

2. Create a table that has the parent-child information:

   The following is the sample code and the insert statement:

   ```
   CREATE   COLUMN TABLE "DEMO"."CCTR_HIE"(
   "CC_CHILD" NVARCHAR(4),
   "CC_PARENT" NVARCHAR(4));
   insert into "DEMO"."CCTR_HIE" values('','')
   insert into "DEMO"."CCTR_HIE" values('C11','c1');
   insert into "DEMO"."CCTR_HIE" values('C12','c1');
   insert into "DEMO"."CCTR_HIE" values('C13','c1');
   insert into "DEMO"."CCTR_HIE" values('C14','c2');
   insert into "DEMO"."CCTR_HIE" values('C21','c2');
   insert into "DEMO"."CCTR_HIE" values('C22','c2');
   insert into "DEMO"."CCTR_HIE" values('C31','c3');
   insert into "DEMO"."CCTR_HIE" values('C1','c');
   insert into "DEMO"."CCTR_HIE" values('C2','c');
   insert into "DEMO"."CCTR_HIE" values('C3','c');
   ```

3. We will put the preceding table into our data foundation of the attribute view as follows:

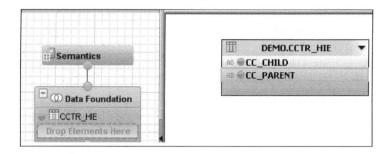

4. Make CC_CHILD the key attribute.

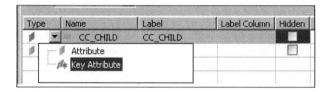

5. Now let's create a new hierarchy as shown in the following screenshot:

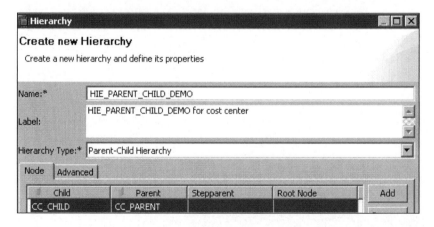

6. Save and activate the hierarchy.

7. Create a new analytical view and add the HIE_PARENT_CHILD_DEMO view and the CCTR_COST table in data foundation.

8. Join CCTR to CCTR_CILD with many is to one relationship. Make sure that in the semantic node, COST is set as a measure.

9. **Save** and **Activate** the analytical view.
10. Preview the data.

As per business needs, we can use one of the two hierarchies along with attribute view or analytical view.

Self-study questions

1. Is text search in SAP HANA different from TREX (SAP NetWeaver search and classification)?

2. While creating hierarchy, what does the Aggregate All Nodes option mean?

3. How can you generate a sales report for a region in a particular currency when you have the sales data in a database table in a different currency?

Summary

In this chapter, we took a deep dive into Full Text Search, fuzzy logic, and hierarchies concepts. We learned how to create and use text search and fuzzy logic. The parent-child and level hierarchies were discussed in detail with a hands-on approach for both.

In the next chapter, we will learn how to work with additional capabilities of SAP HANA such as decision tables and currency conversion. Also, we will learn how our SAP HANA artifacts can be transported across the landscape.

7
Using Decision Tables and Transporting SAP HANA Content

In this chapter, we will learn how to work with additional capabilities of SAP HANA, such as decision tables and currency conversion. We will also learn how our SAP HANA artifacts can be transported across the landscape.

After completing this chapter, you should be able to:

- Create and use a decision table
- Create currency conversion logic
- Transport SAP HANA content across the landscape

What is a decision table?

It is a table representing a complete set of conditional expressions where expressions are mutually exclusive in a predefined area. An example of a decision table is shown in the following figure:

	Conditions/ Course of Action	Rules					
		1	2	3	4	5	6
Condition Studs	Employee type	S	S	S	S	S	S
	Hours worked	<40	<40	<40	<40	>40	>40
	Pay bases salary						
Action Studs	Calculate housing usage		X		X		X
	Calculate overtime						X
	Produce Absence Report		X				

Decision table

Why use decision tables?

Decision tables in general have the following capabilities:

* Powerful visualization
* Compact and structured presentation
* Easier error prevention
* Avoidance of incompleteness and inconsistency
* Modular knowledge organization
* Ability to group related rules into a single table
* Ability to combine the tables to achieve a decision

The same usage can be extended to SAP HANA as well:

* We can use it to implement business rules
* It can help bring business agility

- To to create decision tables in sap HANA
- Calculation view with decision table

A Decision table is a way of implementing business rules in SAP HANA. Having captured the operational decisions, they can be turned into code using the decision tables. Business rules are written on either master data (such as customers, vendor, products) or on transactional data (who bought what and when), and many times on both.

An example of an area where we can use decision tables is customer call centers, when a customer asks for the best plan as per his consumption pattern. Similarly, in the field of banking or health care, we can use decision tables. There are many more areas where decision tables can be used.

SAP HANA has a feature that allows the representation of the business rule included directly into SAP HANA STUDIO. The graphical editor for decision tables creation presents a data foundation node and a decision table node. Tables and information models can be included in the data foundation node while business rules are defined in the decision table node.

In the data foundation, we can include all three views (**attribute**, **analytical**, and **calculation**), the database tables, and the table types.

Vocabulary can include attributes (also calculated attribute) and the parameters. These parameters and attributes are then used to define the business rules, which are checked as condition and relevant Action associated with it are performed. Action could be, only simulation or direct update. So a good vocabulary is the most important part of our decision tree, as it forms the building block of the decision table.

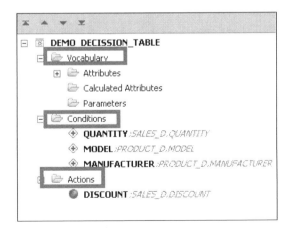

Activation of the decision table generates an SQLscript procedure as a runtime artifact. You can find the generated procedure in the catalog | **_SYS_BIC** schema | **Procedure** folder. It will be `<package-name>/<decisiontable-name>`.

It can be called like any other SQLscript procedure. We just need to make sure that all the conditions that correspond to the parameters of the vocabulary are passed as input parameters to the procedure call. For example:

```
SQL
call "_SYS_BIC"."DEMO/DEMO_DECISSION_TABLE"('100A','XYZ','20');
```

We will follow the following steps to create and consume a decision table:

Create decision table | Edit it **Data Foundation** | Set the **Business Rules** | Consume the table.

Let's create a decision table with the same steps as discussed earlier.

Ours Scenario - Create business rule based on manufacturer, quantity and model. Depending on these factors we will give discounts. We will create the decision table for the same, so that the process is automated.

1. Create the decision table in SAP HANA Studio.

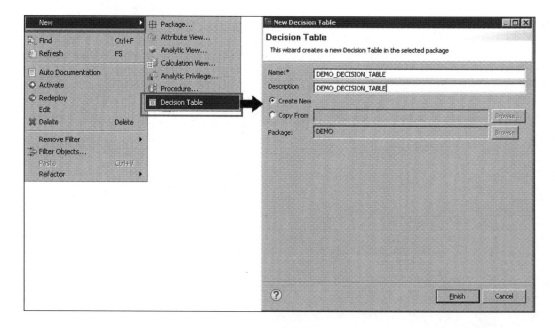

2. Select the table for **Data foundation**. I have chosen **SALES_D** and **PRODUCT_D** (tables available on Packt Publishing website).

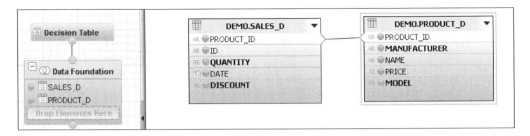

3. Add attributes as shown in the following screenshot:

   QUANTITY and **DISCOUNT** from **SALES_D** table and **MANUFACTURER** and **MODEL** from **PRODUCT_D**. Join **PRODUCT_ID** to **PRODUCT_ID**, as a reference join.

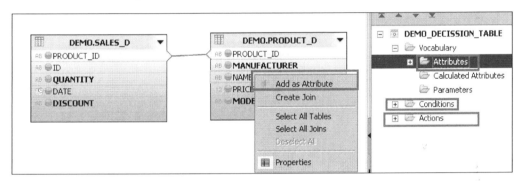

4. Add the attributes as **Conditions** and **Actions** as shown next:

   Here I am making **MANUFACTURER**, **QUANTITY**, and **MODEL** as the condition, as the discount would be based on all these three factors.

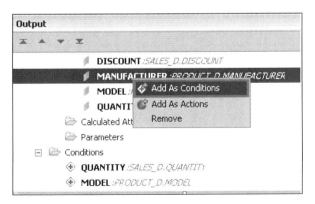

5. Now let's go to the decision table node and set the condition and relevant action:

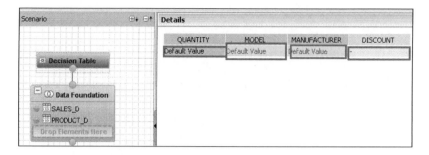

6. We need to click individually on each marked tab and we get the following pop up to fill the values:

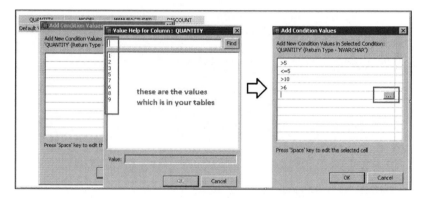

Similarly, for the **MODEL** column:

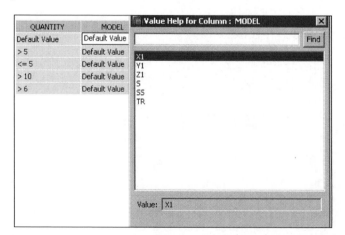

And now our decision table looks like this following image:

QUANTITY	MODEL	MANUFACTURER	DISCOUNT
Default Value	X1	XYZ	10
> 5	S5	ABC	6
<= 5	TR	ABC	11
> 10	Y1	XYZ	18
> 6	Z1	XYZ	15

Please make sure that we have given GRANT SELECT rights to _SYS_REPO schema

```
GRANT SELECT ON SCHEMA DEMO TO _SYS_REPO WITH GRANT OPTION.
```

Save and Activate. Now you can test it by making a call to the generated procedure. To mark the difference, first look at the tables **PRODUCT_D** and **SALES_D** and record the discount field. Now make a call to the decision table and again note the discount field. You will see the difference.

```
SQL
call "_SYS_BIC"."DEMO/DEMO_DECISSION_TABLE"('100A','XYZ','20');
```

While designing the decision table, it is of utmost important to know the scenario and purpose for the business rules. In general, compared to the use of parameters, business rules modeled on decision tables—based on tuples—can update millions of records efficiently in real time, and the impact can be directly accessed by the applications where decisions have to be made in a changing market.

Transport management in SAP HANA

Nobody wants to redevelop the same stuff in the same landscape (many times not even in other landscapes), irrespective of the products. The same applies for SAP HANA as well. Effective management of the content changes across a SAP HANA-based system landscape requires a transport management system.

SAP offers three specific transport techniques for different approaches to SAP HANA content development. SAP HANA provides the following transport management options to choose from, depending on the scenario and the use case:

Use case	Transport management
Native SAP HANA content	SAP HANA application lifecycle management: • Stand-alone transport management of SAP HANA • No ABAP footprint required • Lightweight and easy to use
Native SAP HANA content or part of some solution (BI, Mobile)	Enhanced CTS+: • Transports like any other Non-ABAP content • Integrates in exiting transport landscape • Can be integrated with ChaRM and QGM
SAP HANA content exclusively for ABAP (ABAP for SAP HANA)	HANA transport container • Transports like standard ABAP transports • Integrates in exiting transport landscape • Can be integrated with ChaRM and QGM

In the SAP HANA environment, we can transport the following objects:

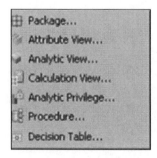

One thing that we should keep in mind is the difference between the design time and the runtime objects. The **Content** folder in the system view is used to manage the various design time objects, while the **Catalog** folder contains the deployment/ activation of the design time object as runtime object.

SAP HANA too has a typical basic landscape consisting of the DEV | QAS | PROD systems.

SAP **HANA Transport Container (HTC)** – A lot of new SAP HANA related optimization has been delivered with SAP Netweaver 740 platform for ABAP development (application). SAP HANA Transport container is one of these. We can leverage SAP HANA transport containers (HTC) for ABAP for SAP HANA content.

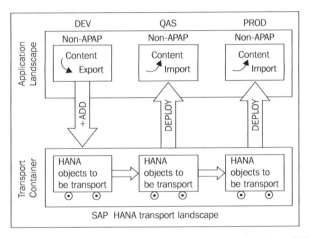

Typical landscape for SAP HANA transport **SAP HANA Transport Container (HTC)** – Landscape.

Let's have a look at the widely used transport mechanisms – SAP HALM and the Export/Import tool one by one.

SAP HANA application lifecycle manager

SAP HANA application lifecycle manager is a stand-alone tool that can be utilized to transport the content from the source system to the target system. Let's see how we can move the SAP HANA content using SAP HALM.

> **Prerequisite**: We assume that the systems and the transport route in CTS is configured. Please contact your basis administrator, if it's not configured.

If you use a CTS+ system without AS JAVA, you also have to enable CTS+ on all the source and target systems. This configuration is done in the SAP HANA application lifecycle management (HALM). We will learn how to do it through the following steps:

1. In the source system, open HALM on your development system. The URL is `https://<Server>:80<instancenumber>/sap/hana/xs/lm`.

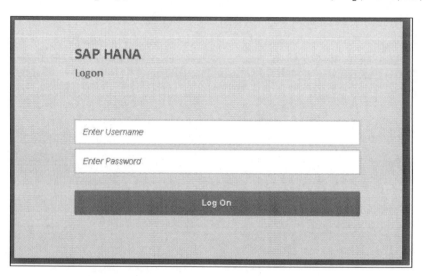

2. After you provide the login credentials, you will get the following screen:

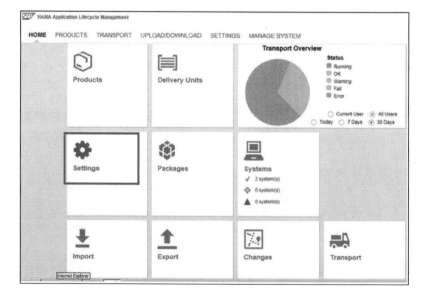

3. Choose the **SETTINGS** tab:

4. Select **Enable CTS Transport | Configure CTS System**:

When you first open this screen, **Enable Native SAP HANA Transport** is selected as the default setting for transports. Changing this setting implies that you cannot use **Native SAP HANA Transport** in this system until you change the setting back again.

5. Enter **Host** and **HTTP(S) Port** of your CTS system:

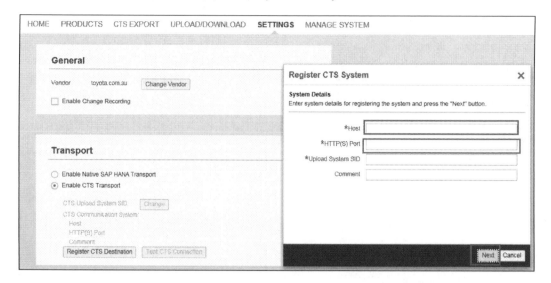

Here, always enter the SID under which this system is known in CTS (the SID that you created when adding the development system to TMS).

6. The next screen asks you to **Maintain Destination**:

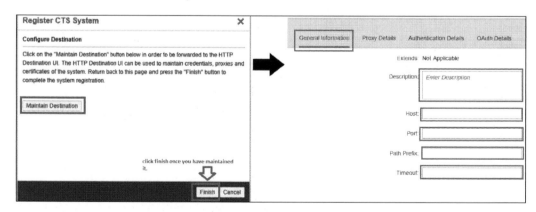

7. Maintain the authentication data:

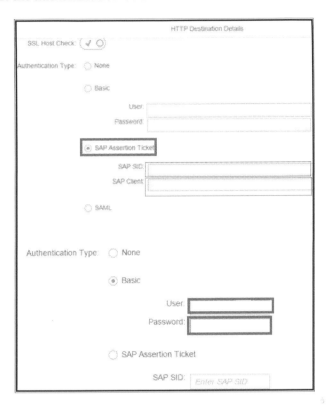

8. Save and close the pop up.

9. You can finish and **Test CTS connection** now.

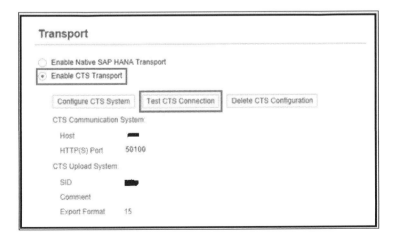

10. Now we need to configure the target systems. Repeat the preceding steps 1, 2, 3, and 4 in the target system.

Our transport management prerequisites are complete and now we can transport in the SAP HANA landscape.

Transporting a delivery unit with HALM

We already learned in the previous chapters about how to create a package and assign a delivery unit. So we will not redo it. We will follow the following steps to Transport a Delivery Unit with HALM:

1. Assign a delivery unit to CTS | Export the Delivery Unit | Release the transport request | Import the transport request.

> Assign a delivery unit that you want to transport to CTS. Open HALM (dev system) **CTS Export** Delivery Units click on **Assign Delivery Units:**

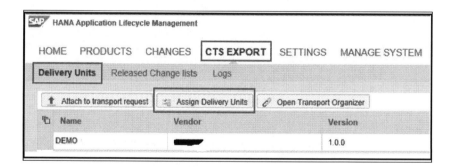

This is a one time configuration. All the other DUs which are not marked can not be transported any more, even with the HALM native environment.

Please select the Delivey Unit which you want to transport. Put a check mark under Assigned to CTS, as shown in the following screenshot:

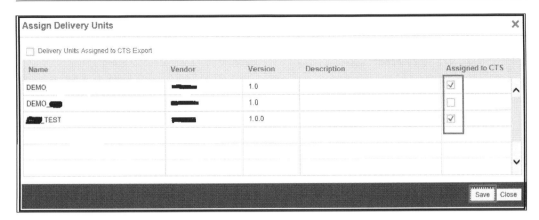

2. Export the delivery unit.

3. Go to **CTS Export | Delivery Unit | Attach to Transport request**:

Next, go to **Start CTS Export**:

For more details, you can go to **Transport Organizer UI** and see it. You can see the logs under **CTS EXPORT**:

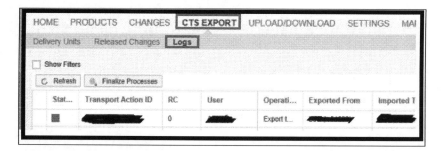

4. Release the transport request:

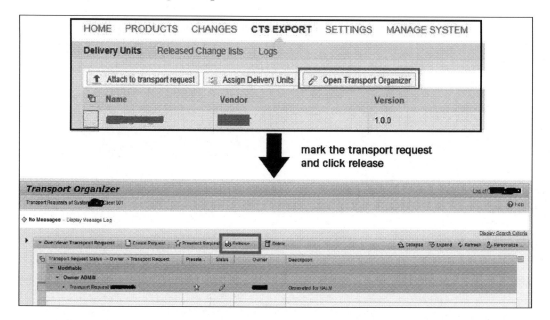

mark the transport request
and click release

It asks you to confirm the release of the transport request. Confirm it.

5. Import the transport request.

You can go to your CTS system and in your import queue, you will see the transport request. Choose the request and import it.

This completes our transport via HALM.

Similarly, you can transport the change lists with HALM.

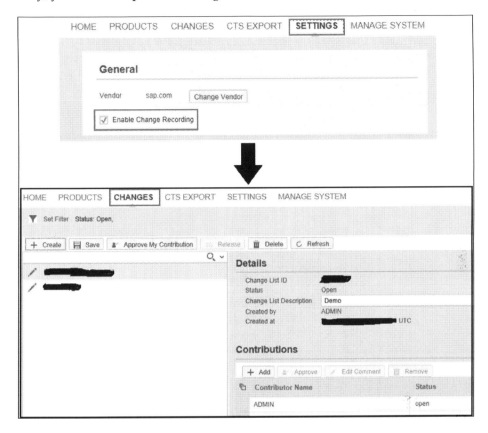

Here you can work with your change list object, mark it, and later release it to be transported with CTS.

If the delivery unit is assigned to CTS, you can transport it with SAP HANA Studio as well. Make sure you are at SAP HANA SPS08 and above. To start the export via CTS in the SAP HANA development perspective, click with the right mouse button. Choose **Export**. We will not go into detail, as it is beyond the scope of this book. A good idea would be to follow the graphical interface and the guide from SAP:

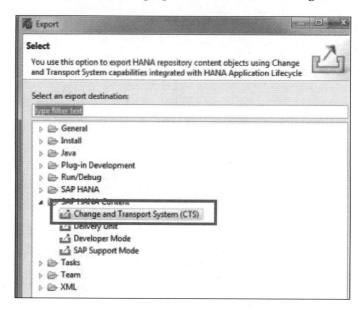

Export and import – moving SAP HANA content manually

It's one of the simpler ways of moving the SAP HANA contents (information models, tables, and landscapes) in the landscape. It also supports the import of Meta Data from the other systems.

It can be accessed from **Quick Launch | Content**; or through the **File** menu; By the right-click **Context** menu option of tables.

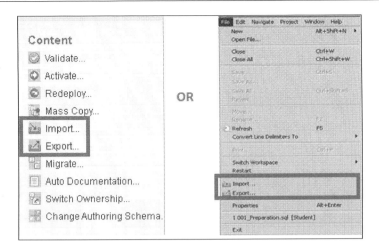

While **Export,** you get the following options to choose, as shown in the screenshot:

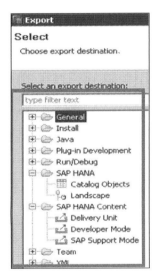

For **SAP HANA Content**, we can choose from:

- **Delivery Unit**: While doing Export, it is a single unit which can be mapped to multiple packages but exported as a single entity, so that all the packages assigned to the delivery unit can be treated as a single unit.

- **Developer Mode**: This option can be used to export individual objects (views) to a location in the local system. This can be used only in rare cases.

- **SAP Support Mode**: This can be used to export the objects along with the data for SAP support purposes. This can be used when requested. For example, suppose a user creates a view which throws up an error and he is unable to resolve it. In such a case, he can use this option to export the view along with the data and share it with SAP for debugging purposes.

From **SAP HANA**, we can choose the following contents:

- **Landscape**: This option can be used to export the landscape from one system to the other

- **Tables**: This option can be used to export the tables along with their content Similarly, when we choose **Import**, one may get the following options:

With **Import** you get the following options to choose, as shown in the following screenshot:

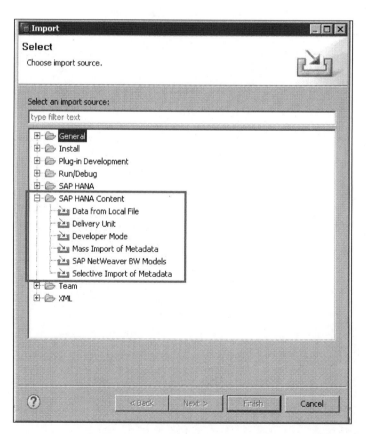

From **SAP HANA Content**, From SAP HANA Content, as can be seen in the preceding screen capture, we can choose one of the following:

- **Delivery Unit**: The exported delivery unit can be imported either from the HANA server or from the local client location

- **Developer Mode**: It is used to import the already exported views from the local client location

- **Mass Import of Metadata**: This option can be used to import the meta data (table definition) from the SAP ERP source systems, using SAP Load Controller, into HANA, if the user uses Sybase Replication Server for Data Provisioning

- **Selective Import of Meta Data**: This is similar to the previous option but in this case, SAP BO Data Services will be used for Data Provisioning

Data from Local File was discussed in *Chapter 3, Different Ways of SAP HANA Data Load*.

From **SAP HANA Studio**, we can choose:

- **Landscape**: To import the exported landscape in the target system
- **Tables**: To import the exported tables into the target system

Let's try our hand with the **Export/Import** process.

For the export process, we follow the following steps (I am showing it with **Delivery Unit**):

1. Choose **Delivery Unit** under **SAP HANA Content**.
2. Choose the **System for exports**.
3. We choose the **Delivery Unit** that we want to **Export**.
4. We can include the list of packages inside the Delivery Unit.

5. Choose the **Export** location. It can be any of the three as shown next:

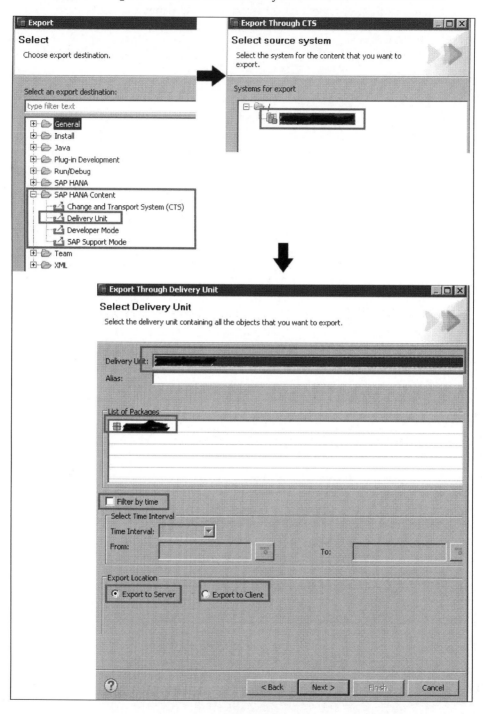

Select Time Interval – The user can restrict the export through Filter by time which means that only the views which are modified within the specified time interval will be exported.

Export to server – The exported files would be stored on Server.

Export to client gives us an option to choose the location where we should save it in the client system(your desktop/Laptop).

Attach to Transport Request – It allows you to add it to transport request, so that you can move it across the landscpe.

Once we are done with the preceding steps, we get a confirmation summary for the final verification. Once we confirm, the export is triggered.

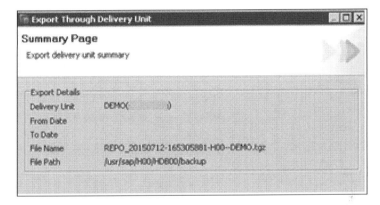

 Instead of choosing **Delivery Mode,** you can choose **Developer Mode**: **Quick Launch | Content | Export | Developer Mode | Next**.

Select the views to be exported. One can select any of the HANA artifact (single entity) or collection of Views and packages. The **Export** location could be chosen as local client or server. Then click on **Finish** to complete the process.

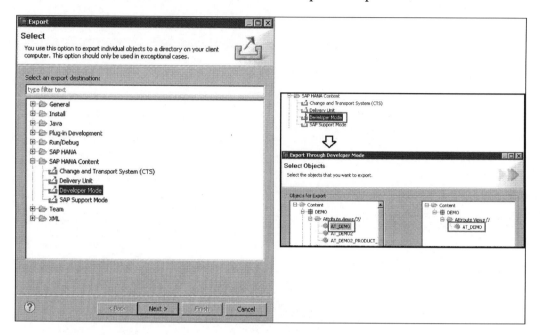

Similarly, like Developer mode and Delivery mode, we can also use **SAP Support Mode**:

Select the view that needs to be debugged by the SAP support. This will export the view along with the table data it refers to. This will be directly exported to the HANA Server backup location.

Let's now see the Import process.

Again, I am choosing **Delivery Unit**, as I exported the delivery unit. Following are the main steps:

Quick Launch | Content | Import | Delivery Unit | Next | Select the **Delivery Unit** (from HANA Server /local client).

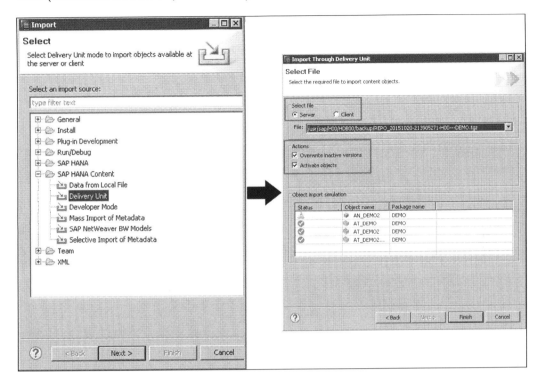

We can select **Overwrite inactive versions** which means that if there are any inactive versions of objects (from the previous import) that exist, then those will be overwritten.

We can also choose to select **Activate objects**. Once the import is complete, all the imported objects will be activated by default. The user does not need to trigger the activation manually for the imported views.

Instead of choosing **Delivery Mode,** you can choose **Developer Mode** for import:

Quick Launch | Content | Import | Developer Mode | Next | Browse the Local Client location where the views are exported | Select the views to be imported | **Finish**.

Here also, the user can select **Overwrite Existing Objects** to overwrite the already imported objects, if any.

We also have an option of doing **Mass Import of Metadata**: **Quick Launch | Content | Import | Mass Import of Metadata | Next |** Select the target system.

 Prerequisite: System for Mass Import should be configured, otherwise you will get the following error message:

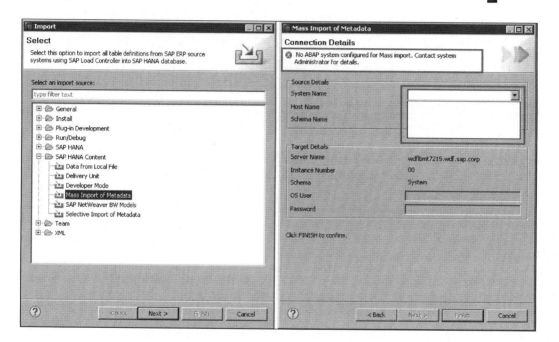

Import of **Landscape** and **Tables** can be done in the same way.

Currency conversion in SAP HANA

A global company, with sales in different currencies, might like to have consistency in the display data and would prefer a single currency for aggregation purposes. Say, for example, a hotel booking site would show the price and allow the customer to book the rooms in the customer's local currency (whichever part of the world he is in). But internally, the system has to take care of the conversion of all the prices as per local currency of the hotel.

So taking care of currency conversion becomes an important aspect of data modelling and reporting in SAP HANA. Other SAP products, such as SAP BW, also provide currency conversion functionality at a transformation and reporting level. SAP BPC too provides the currency conversion functionality using the RATE application. SAP Integrated Planning (IP) provides the standard function for currency conversion. So a user from any of the mentioned SAP backgrounds will easily co-relate to the concept.

Let's learn in the following steps, the process of currency conversion in SAP HANA.

> **Prerequisite**: Check if the currency conversion related tables (TCUR*) are present in our schema and have data, otherwise ask the SAP basis team to replicate the tables into the schema.

The tables to be checked are:

Table	Usage
TCURR	For exchange rate
TCURV	For exchange rate types for currency translation
TCURF	Conversion factor
TCURN	Quotations
TCURX	Currency decimal

> Create an analytical view | Create **Measure** | Enable for conversion | Choose **Target Currency** | Choose source currency | Define date and exchange type.

We can create the target currency with a fixed currency or with an input parameters/column. We will start with the fixed target currency and then will later see the additional steps for input parameters.

1. **Create an analytical view**: Name the analytical view as **AN_CURR** with description as a fixed currency. (I'm not showing you the steps of creating an analytical view, as by now you would have mastered it.) Add the physical table **EPM_MODEL.SNWD_SO** to **Data Foundation**. (We will use the standard data provided by SAP as EPM model.)

Good practice would be to create a separate schema with all the relevant table currency (such as **TCUR**) and use it. For this analytical view, we could, if we have separate currency schema, assign default schema as **TCUR**:

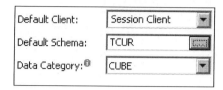

2. In **Data Foundation,** add columns to the output:

```
SO_ID (Sales Order Number)
CURRENCY_CODE
GROSS_AMOUNT
```

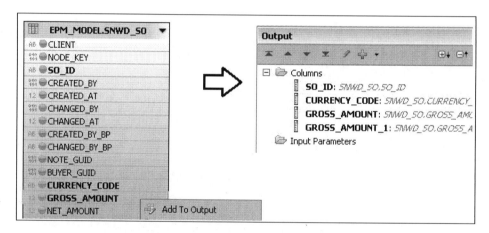

We will add **GROSS_AMOUNT** twice as we will use it for different currencies.

3. In the semantics node, mark **SO_ID** as the attribute; **GROSS_AMOUNT** as **Measure**; and **GROSS_SAOUNT_1** and **CURRENCY_CODE** as attribute.

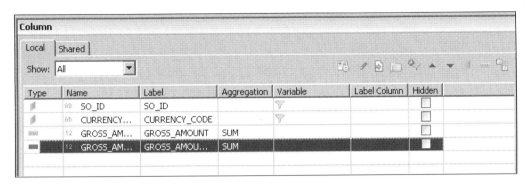

4. Since we have two **GROSS_AMOUNT**, we will rename them. One for the source currency and the other one for the target. Rename the **Measure** **GROSS_AMOUNT** to **GROSS_AMOUNT_EUR** and **GROSS_AMOUNT_1** to **GROSS_AMOUNT_USD**.

5. Go to the **Assign Semantic** tab (as shown in the following screenshot) and click on it:

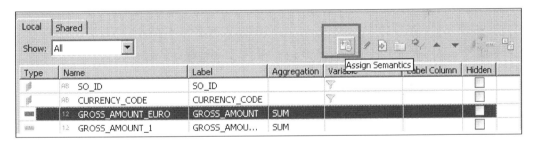

6. You will get the following screen:

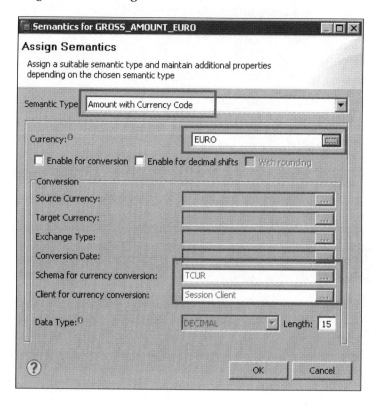

7. Change **Semantic Type** of this **Measure** to **Amount** with **Currency Code**. Set **Currency** to **Fixed Type EUR**. Do not select **Enable for Conversion** or **Decimal Shifts**.

Now we need to include the gross amount field again for USD. So we will again do the currency conversion logic, as shown in the following screenshot:

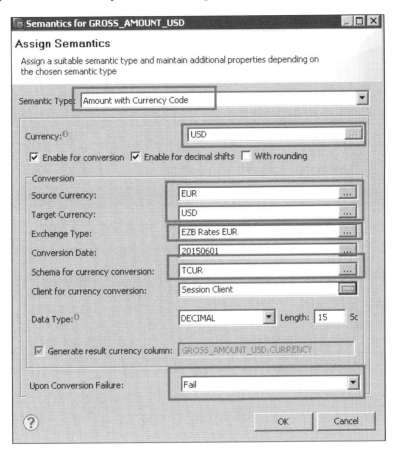

8. Fill the values as shown in the preceding screenshot. Make sure the client for **Currency Conversion** is set to **800**. Set **Upon Conversion Failure** as **Fail**.

We can change the client setting by using the change client tab. It will give us the following screenshot:

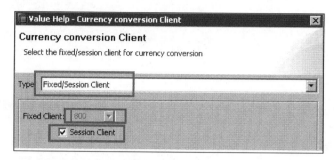

9. **Save** and **Activate** the **Analytic View**.

10. Perform **Data Preview** and make note on the **Raw Data** tab.

You will now see your two **Measures**: **GROSS_AMOUNT_EUR** as well as the converted **GROSS_AMOUNT_USD**.

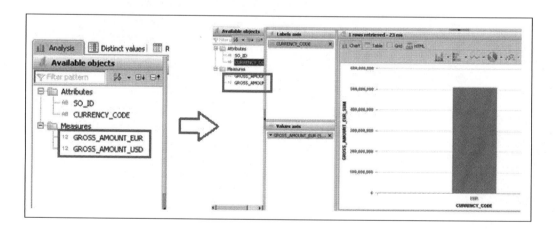

Coming to another aspect of it, say for example you want to give an option of variable or input parameters to the user, while choosing the target currency instead of having fixed values. Let's see how the input parameter would be created.

1. Create a new input parameter in the output area:

2. Fill in the details as shown next.

Use **Parameter Type** as **Direct**; this gives you the option for selecting semantic type as currency, date, or blank. And you get the option according to system. For example, if you select **Currency** then the system will provide you a list of currencies for the variable value selection, but if you select nothing then during the variable value selection, no help values will be available and you will have to provide the variable value manually.

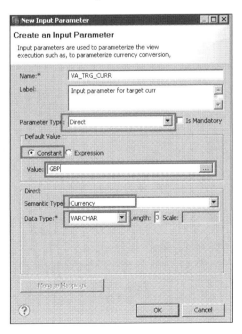

Similarly, you can create the input parameter for date:

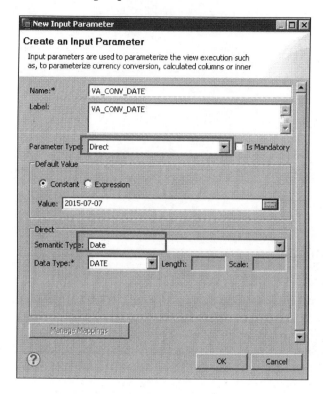

You can also have the exchange rate as the input parameter or the variable.

You can then use it in the calculated columns as variable inputs rather than fixed ones, as shown in the following screenshot:

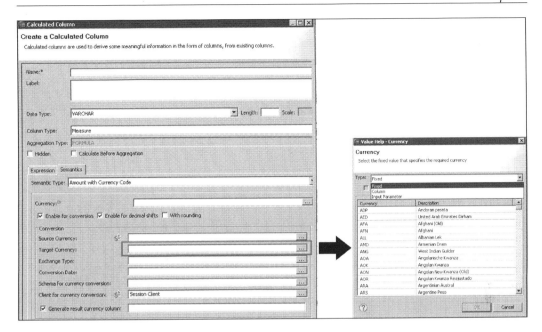

You choose input parameter and you will see all that we previously created:

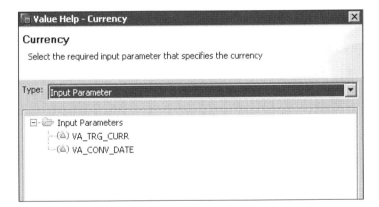

This completes our discussion on currency conversion.

Self-study questions

1. Can you think of business areas in your company where a decision table could be of help?

2. Analyze your transport mechanism and justify which technique would be suitable for its needs.

3. Find a detailed report of the decision table.

4. Try to change the layout of the decision table that you created earlier.

Summary

In this chapter, we learned about how we can create a decision table and automate the business rule, in detail. We also had a look at the various benefits of using it. Transport management being an important aspect of HANA content management across a landscape, we worked on the various concepts related to HALM and export/import in this chapter. In the last section of the chapter, we built on currency conversion logic and used it in our view. This brings us to the end of creating artifact and other modelling content in SAP HANA.

In the next chapter, we will be reporting with SAP HANA data models. We will use our own data models created in the previous chapters for reporting. Also, we will take a general overview of all the tools available in SAP HANA. For a practical exercise, our focus will be on only two tools - design studio and analysis for office.

8

Consuming SAP HANA Data Models

Until the previous chapter we were working on the Information model, and you learned their prerequisites and how to create them. In this chapter, we will learn how to report with SAP HANA data models and use our own data models created in the previous chapter for reporting. Also, we will have a general overview of all the tools available in SAP HANA.

After completing this chapter you should be able to:

- Connect to SAP HANA
- Reporting tools for SAP HANA
- Create reporting use case for Analysis for Office
- Create reporting use case for SAP BO Design Studio

Connecting to the SAP HANA database

SAP HANA supports various connectivity choices. These can be categorized as follows:

- **BI Consumer Services (BICS)**: This is the SAP Proprietary interface that offers advantages for OLAP access over MDX on multidimensional reporting objects.
- **Open Database connectivity (ODBC)**: This is widely used across the industry. Database requests are made via SQL.
- **Java Database connectivity (JDBC)**: This is mostly popular with the Unix platform used for relational reporting

- **ODBO**: OLE DB for OLAP-MDX, multi-dimensional expression, is used to send the request

The following illustration shows the different connectivity options supported for frontend tools connecting to SAP HANA:

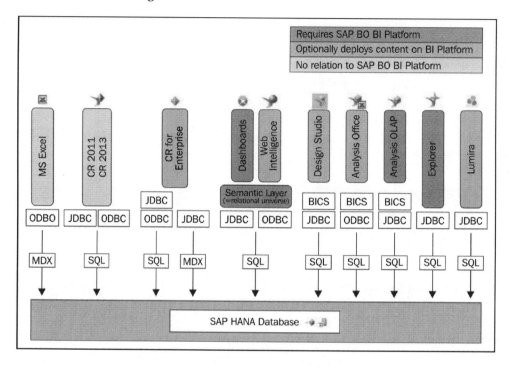

Reporting tools for SAP HANA

The modelling artifact created on SAP HANA Studio can be accessed in Studio itself. But most of the time these views are consumed as a report for different business scenarios by a non-technical end user or a user who is from a business area. So to facilitate smoother and less technical reporting interface, we connect separate reporting tools to SAP HANA.

SAP supports a large number of tools that can be used for reporting in SAP HANA. SAP suggests using the SAP business objects BI suite, which includes SAP Business Objects crystal reports, Analysis Office, and Explorer. It supports other tools as well. It should be noted that we use only tools that can create and consume MDX queries and data.

Let's try to learn a few of the tools and their usage.

Analysis for Office

Analysis for Office is used to report from the analytical view or the calculation view.

We can have multiple views from different HANA systems in one workbook or sheet.

With SAP BO Analysis for Office we can:

- Analyze data with the design panel
- Filter members
- Sort data by measures
- Insert charts and filter components
- Convert crosstab cells to formula
- Create presentations
- Save/open workbook to/from the SAP BI Platform server

Here, we will be using a local ODBC connection for analysis in office and to access the HANA view.

 A prerequisite is that the ODBC connection already be created by the administrator.

The following are the steps to access our HANA Artifacts via analysis for office:

1. Open Analysis for Office application.
2. Navigate to **Analysis TAB | Insert Data Source.**

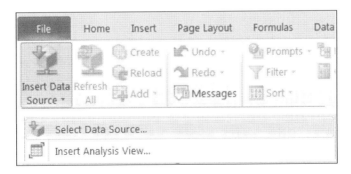

3. In order to use a local ODBC connection (instead of authenticating against BOE and using a relational DB connection published to CMC), click on **Skip**.

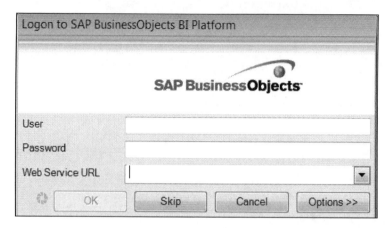

4. Once you click skip, it takes you to the **Select Data Source** screen:

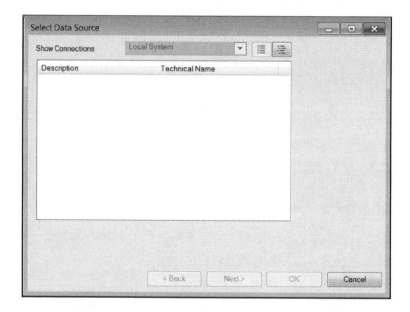

Here, it's empty, but you will see sources in your landscape and you can choose the source.

5. It then prompts you for HANA SB credentials:

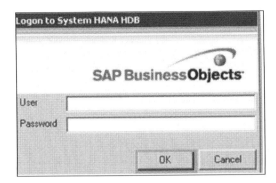

6. Now you are directed to the package you have access to in SAP HANA. Choose the view you want from your package.

7. A report based on the view is shown and you can play around with various measures and dimensions to build your report.

SAP Business Objects Analysis for OLAP

SAP Business Objects Analysis is a web-based application used for the ad-hoc OLAP client for business users to analyze OLAP data. It can also be used to report from calculation view and analytical view. Analysis for OLAP is available inside the BI Launchpad.

Before we can use it, we have to create the OLAP connections.

This can be done using the following steps:

1. Log on to **Central Management Console**, choose **OLAP Connections** and fill in the details as shown in the following screenshot:

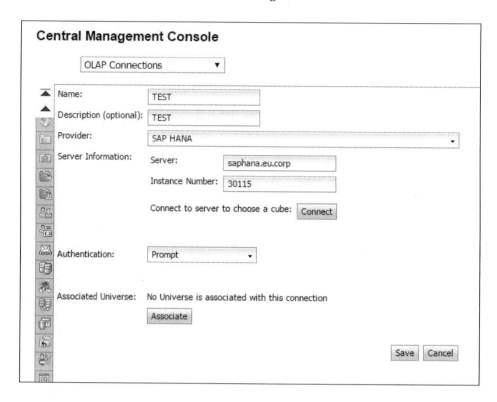

2. Log on to the BI Launchpad and under **Applications**, choose **Analysis edition for OLAP**.

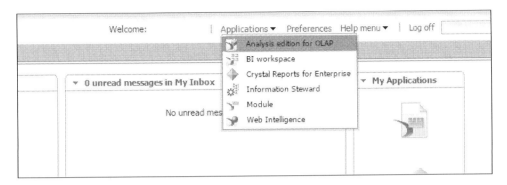

3. You get the new analysis workspace, and in the **Analyze** tab, you can search for your data source.

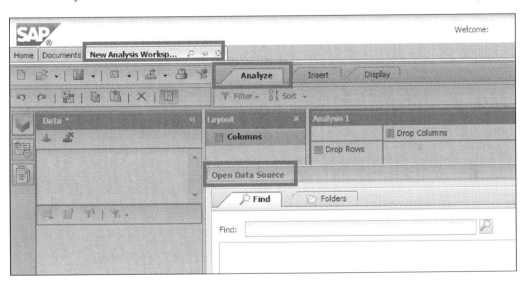

4. This opens your view here. If you are using a SAP BO design studio and want to consume your HANA view in design studio.

5. Go to **Design Studio | Add Data Source**, provide the connection details, and you can connect to the view in SAP BO design studio.

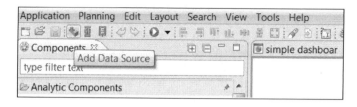

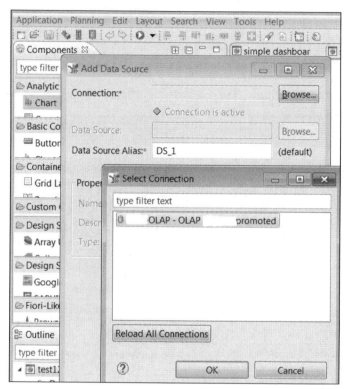

Using Microsoft Excel as a reporting tool

Typically, customers / end users use different reporting tools in a business environment. But since Microsoft is widely used across user groups, it let's you see how we can expose our SAP HANA information model via Microsoft Excel.

The following are the steps to access the HANA views on Microsoft Excel:

1. Go to Microsoft Excel 2010 or above.

2. Go to **Data | From Other Sources | From Data Connection Wizard**.

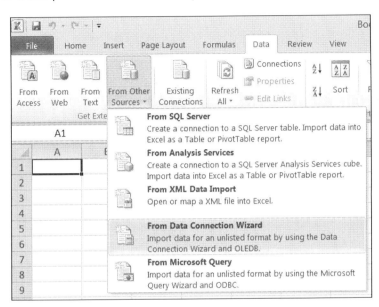

3. From the data connection wizard, choose **Other/Advanced**:

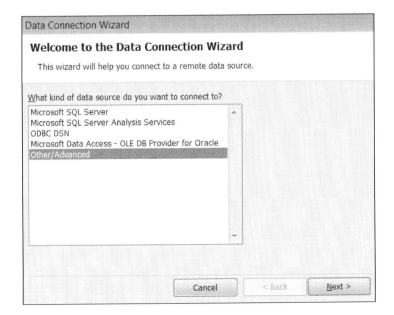

4. In the next pop up, it asks you to choose the **SAP HANA MDX Provider** option and logging credentials for SAP HANA:

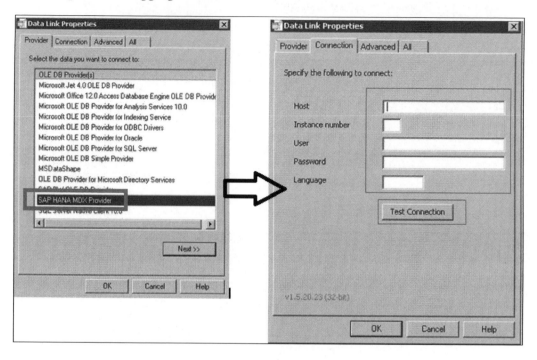

Click on **Test Connection** and then click on **OK**.

5. Now, we can select the database and the specific view we want for reporting:

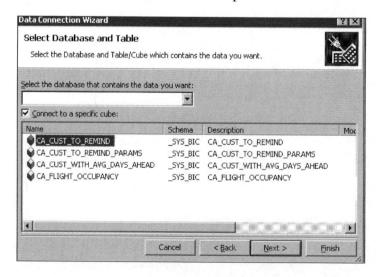

6. We can save this connection with a friendly name:

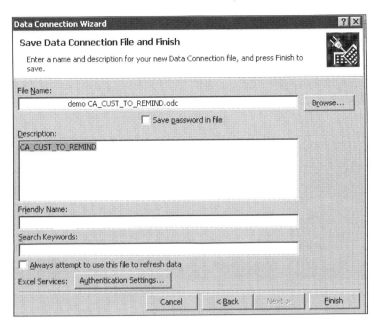

7. Excel opens up with a pivot table; click on **OK**, it asks you for the HANA server credentials:

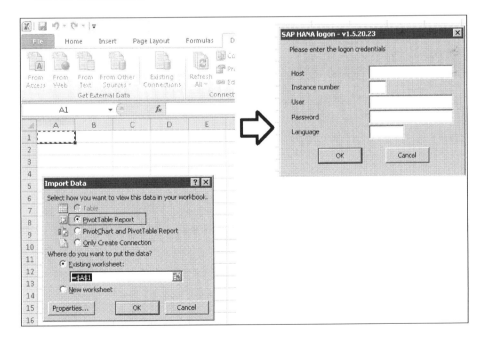

8. You can play around with the fields that you want to see in the report and display the report accordingly:

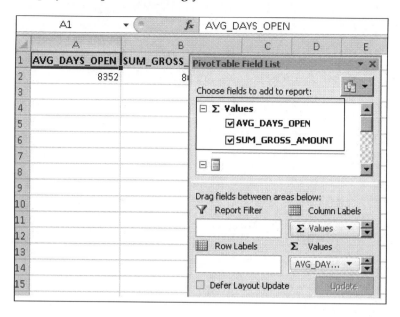

There are other reporting tools as well which can be used, such as Lumira, SAP BO dashboard, and explorer.

Summary

After reading this chapter, you should be able to understand the connectivity option for reporting in SAP HANA, and understand the SAP business object reporting possibilities. You also learned how to create a pivot table in Microsoft Excel by querying SAP HANA, learn connectivity with Office for Analysis, and how SAP BO analysis for OLAP can be used for ad hoc reporting.

This chapter brings us to the end of the reporting topic and SAP HANA artifacts. In the next chapter, we will take an introductory look at the various library functions that SAP HANA has. We will explore how these library functions can be beneficial for us. You will also learn about the prerequisite for using these library functions.

An Introduction to Application Function Library

9

In this last chapter, we will be introduced to various library functions that SAP HANA has. We will look at its benefits and the various aspects related to it. We will also see what the predelivered, commonly utilized business and predictive algorithms are.

After completing this chapter, you should be able to:

- Understand the application function library
- Understand the predictive analysis library
- Use the business function library

One of the core concepts of SAP HANA is to move application logic into the database, and to do so, it provides several techniques. One of the most important of these techniques is the use of application functions. Application functions are like database procedures written in C++ and are called from outside to perform data-intensive and complex operations. An **Application Function Library** contains the **Predictive Analysis Library** and **Business Function Library** components.

Application Function Library

The SAP HANA application offers various predelivered, commonly utilized business and predictive algorithms. These functionalities are stored in the **Application Function Library (AFL)**. The SAP HANA in-memory computing engine offers various algorithms for in-memory computing. It provides several application libraries for developers, partners, and customers who develop applications that run on SAP HANA. The libraries are linked dynamically to the SAP HANA database kernel. Customers can use these functions to speed up both implementation and performance.

Currently, all AFLs are delivered in one archive (that is, one SAR file with the name AFL<version_string>.SAR). The AFL archive is not part of the SAP HANA appliance, and must be installed separately by an administrator. Please refer to the SAP HANA server installation and update guide.

Predictive Analysis Library

The **Predictive Analysis Library (PAL)** defines functions that can be called from within SQLscript procedures to perform analytic algorithms. It includes the following classic and universal predictive analysis algorithms in nine data mining categories:

- Clustering
- Association
- Statistics
- Classification
- Time series
- Social network analysis
- Regression
- Preprocessing
- Miscellaneous

The algorithms in PAL were carefully selected as most of these algorithms are generally available in other database products. Also, these are frequently used and needed for SAP HANA applications.

The following are the prerequisites for using PAL:

- Install the latest SAP HANA SPS
- Install the **AFL**, which includes the PAL
- Enable the script server in the HANA instance. SAP note 1,650,957 describes its steps.

The revision of the AFL must match the revision of SAP HANA.

Calling PAL functions

To use PAL functions, you must do the following:

1. From within the SQLscript code, generate a procedure that wraps the PAL function.

   Any user granted with the `AFLPM_CREATOR_ERASER_EXECUTE` role can generate an `AFLLANG` procedure for a specific PAL function. The syntax is shown as follows:

   ```
   CALL SYS.AFLLANG_WRAPPER_PROCEDURE_CREATE ('<area_name>',
   '<function_name>','<schema_name>', '<procedure_name>', <signature_
   table>);
   ```

   The following is a description of the preceding syntax:

   - `<area_name>`: This is always set to `AFLPAL`.
   - `<function_name>`: This is the PAL built-in function name.
   - `<schema_name>`: This is the name of the schema that you want to create.
   - `<procedure_name>`: This is the name of the PAL procedure (any name as per our choice).
   - `<signature_table>`: This is a user-defined table variable. The table contains records to describe the position.

2. Call the procedure, for example, from an SQLscript procedure.

   After generating a PAL procedure, any user that has the `AFL__SYS_AFL_AFLPAL_EXECUTE` role can call the procedure, using the syntax as follows:

   ```
   SYS.AFLLANG_WRAPPER_PROCEDURE_CREATE ('<area_name>',
   '<function_name>','<schema_name>', '<procedure_name>', <signature_
   table>);).
   ```

   The following is a description of the preceding syntax:

   - `<schema_name>`: This is the name of the schema where the procedure is located
   - `<procedure_name>`: This is the procedure name specified when generating the procedure in step 1
   - `<data_input_table>`: This is the user-defined name(s) of the procedure's input table(s)
   - `<parameter_table>`: This is the user-defined name of the procedure's parameter table. The table structure is described in the parameter table structure

     °   `<output_table>`: This is the user-defined name(s) of the procedure's output table(s)

For example, let's see a few of the available algorithms and functions in the Predictive Analysis Library. For a detailed list of all the available algorithms please see `https://help.sap.com/hana/SAP_HANA_Predictive_Analysis_Library_PAL_en.pdf`:

Category	PAL algorithm	Built-in function name
Clustering	Affinity propagation	AP
	Agglomerate hierarchical clustering	HCAGGLOMERATE
	Anomaly detection	ANOMALYDETECTION
	Self-organizing maps	SELFORGMAP
Social network analysis	Link prediction	LINKPREDICTION
Statistics	Distribution fitting	DISTRFIT DISTRFITCENSORED

Business Function Library

The **Business Function Library** (BFL) is one of these application libraries. It contains a prebuilt parameter driven function in the financial area. This library helps us develop compound business algorithms that are fully compliant with the SAP HANA calculation engine. The BFL extends the computation ability of SAP HANA with complex and performance-critical algorithms that are requested by applications.

Some of the areas which gets extended with these library are:

- Utilizing new hardware (for example, multicore, built-in vector engine)
- Massive parallel main memory processing
- Changing the boundaries between the application server and the data management layer
- Usage of extended SQL (SQLscript)
- Rich functionalities in the calculation engine
- Quick application delivery

The following are the prerequisites for using PAL:

- Installation of the latest SAP HANA SPS
- Installation of the **AFL**, which includes the PAL

- Enabling of the script server in the HANA instance. SAP note 1,650,957 describes these steps.

Some of the available functions in the business function library are listed as follows (a complete list can be seen in the SAP HANA developer guide).

Function	Description
Annual depreciation	Calculates annual depreciation according to three common methods.
Cycles	Calculates seasonal factors from Fourier coefficients. It combines sine and cosine waves to help you determine seasonality or other cyclical business factors.
Cumulate	Calculates the cumulative totals in one row based on the original numbers in another row.
Days	Returns the number of days in each period defined by each pair of From and To dates.
Days outstanding	Calculates receipts or payments based on the level of days outstanding.
Delay stock	Calculates purchases required to meet future demand.
Forecast	Combines actual and forecast data to produce a rolling forecast. Eliminates scripting of feeds.
Forecast sensitivity	Returns a calculation for the proportion of requests that will be queued because there were no agents available when the request was answered.
Funds	Calculates the use of funds or the source of funds.
Internal Rate of Return (IRR)	Calculates the internal rate of return for a series of cash flow on specified dates.
Net Present Value (NPV)	Calculates the sum of a series of future cash flow values after discounting each to a present value based on the annual rate input for the period in which it is being calculated.
Rate	Calculates the percentage interest rate per period for an account, given its start balance, end balance, payment amount per period and the number of periods.
Stock flow	Works out the level of supply needed to meet target forecasts for stock cover.
Year-Over-Year Difference	Calculates the year over year difference between the current and previous time periods.
Year to Date	Calculates year to date totals based on original data.
Year-to-Date Statistical	Calculates the original numbers in one row based on the year-to-date figures in another row.

This is not a complete list. Please refer to the SAP HANA developer guide for the complete list.

Related information can be found in the SAP HANA developer guide for SAP HANA Studio.

Self-study questions

1. Can you think of library functions that might be of help in your business scenarios ?

Summary

In this chapter, we were introduced to the application function lifecycle and its benefits. You learned about when to use the business function library and predictive analysis library.

This brings us to the end of the book, By now, you should be comfortable with topics related to real-time analytics. You should now be able to work with SAP HANA SQL, understand different SAP HANA views and their usage, load data in SAP HANA, and create data models in SAP HANA. You should also be aware of various measures to ensure the best performance of reporting through an optimized data model and be able to create reports on it.

Index

E

elements, SQL
data types 2
expressions 3
functions 3
identifiers 2
operators 3
predicates 3
engines, SAP HANA
CALCULATION engine 22
JOIN engine 22
OLAP engine 22
expressions 3
extensions, SQLscript
datatype extension (create/drop type) 7
functional extension (create function) 7
procedural extension (create procedure) 7

F

features, SAP HANA
Insert only on Delta 21
partitioning 20
filters
creating 104
creating, steps 105-108
flat file, SAP HANA
data, loading from 38-44
folder structures, for system view
Backup 30
Catalog 30
Content 30
Provisioning 30
Security 30
Full Text Search
about 131
benefits 133
capabilities 133
creating 131
Fuzzy Search 132
score() function 132
search option, enabling 134, 135
Text Analysis 131

use cases 132
using 131
functions 3
fuzzy search
applied applications 132
data types 133

H

HALM
delivery unit, transporting 158-161
URL 154
HANA- supported scenarios
search-based applications 133
Standard Analytics 133
HANA views
accessing, on Microsoft 189-192
hierarchies
creating 135
level based 80
level hierarchy 135
level hierarchy, creating 136-140
parent-child 80
parent-child hierarchy 135
parent-child hierarchy, creating 141-143

I

identifiers 2
information views, SAP HANA
analytic view 70
attribute view 70
calculation view 70
input parameters
creating 108-111

J

JOINS, in SAP HANA
about 14
referential JOIN 14
spatial JOIN 14
star JOIN 14
temporal JOIN 14

text JOIN 14
versus unions 15

K

key attribute
  defining 79-81

L

late materialization
  about 18
  advantages 19
load balancing 21

M

measure
  about 70
  calculated measure 70
  counters 70
  restricted measures 70
  simple measure 70
Microsoft Excel
  using, as reporting tool 188
modeling artifacts, SAP HANA
  about 23
  principles 24-26

O

OLAP
  SAP Business Objects Analysis 185-187
operators 3

P

packages
  about 32
  creating 32
  deleting 33
parallelization 21
parameters, for creating procedures
  Language 10
  Reads SQL Data 10
  With result view 10

partitioning 20
performance optimization factors, column storage
  block iteration 18
  compression 18
  late materialization 18, 19
  support for parallelism 18
perspectives, SAP HANA Studio
  about 27
  SAP HANA Administration Console 27
  SAP HANA Modeler 27
predicates 3
Predictive Analysis Library (PAL)
  about 193, 194
  functions, calling 195, 196
  functions, URL 196
  prerequisites 194
preferences
  adjusting, steps 71-74
procedures
  about 9
  creating 9
  creating, with SQL editor 9-11
  creating, with wizard 11-13

Q

Quick Launch 82

R

referential JOIN 14
related elements
  calculated attribute, creating 92
  calculated columns, creating 94, 95
  calculated measures, creating 93
  creating 91
  variables, creating 95, 96
restricted measure
  creating 98-103
row storage 17, 18

S

transport management
  in SAP HANA 151-153
  use cases 152

U

unions
  versus JOINS 15
use cases, partitioning
  load balancing 21
  parallelization 21

V

variables
  creating 108-111

W

wizard
  procedures, creating with 11-13

Thank you for buying
Real Time Analytics with SAP HANA

About Packt Publishing

Packt, pronounced 'packed', published its first book, *Mastering phpMyAdmin for Effective MySQL Management*, in April 2004, and subsequently continued to specialize in publishing highly focused books on specific technologies and solutions.

Our books and publications share the experiences of your fellow IT professionals in adapting and customizing today's systems, applications, and frameworks. Our solution-based books give you the knowledge and power to customize the software and technologies you're using to get the job done. Packt books are more specific and less general than the IT books you have seen in the past. Our unique business model allows us to bring you more focused information, giving you more of what you need to know, and less of what you don't.

Packt is a modern yet unique publishing company that focuses on producing quality, cutting-edge books for communities of developers, administrators, and newbies alike. For more information, please visit our website at www.packtpub.com.

About Packt Enterprise

In 2010, Packt launched two new brands, Packt Enterprise and Packt Open Source, in order to continue its focus on specialization. This book is part of the Packt Enterprise brand, home to books published on enterprise software – software created by major vendors, including (but not limited to) IBM, Microsoft, and Oracle, often for use in other corporations. Its titles will offer information relevant to a range of users of this software, including administrators, developers, architects, and end users.

Writing for Packt

We welcome all inquiries from people who are interested in authoring. Book proposals should be sent to author@packtpub.com. If your book idea is still at an early stage and you would like to discuss it first before writing a formal book proposal, then please contact us; one of our commissioning editors will get in touch with you.

We're not just looking for published authors; if you have strong technical skills but no writing experience, our experienced editors can help you develop a writing career, or simply get some additional reward for your expertise.

SAP HANA Cookbook

ISBN: 978-1-78217-762-3   Paperback: 284 pages

Your all-inclusive guide to understanding SAP HANA with practical recipes

1. Understand the architecture of SAP HANA, effectively transforming your business with the modeler and in-memory computing engine.

2. Learn about Business Intelligence, Analytics, and Predictive analytics on top of SAP HANA Models.

3. Gain knowledge on the process of transforming your data to insightful information using the Modeler.

Creating Universes with SAP BusinessObjects

ISBN: 978-1-78217-090-7   Paperback: 310 pages

Create and maintain powerful SAP BusinessObjects Universes with the SAP Information Design Tool

1. Gain all the skills needed to achieve your business intelligence goals by linking your business, data, and people using SAP BusinessObjects.

2. Master the SAP Information Design Tool to create a universe and explore its resources such as the connection, data foundation layer, and business layer.

3. Learn to use a business case supported with illustrated diagrams that will help you to build robust universes.

Please check **www.PacktPub.com** for information on our titles

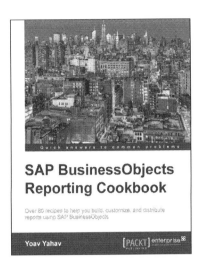

SAP BusinessObjects Reporting Cookbook

ISBN: 978-1-78217-243-7   Paperback: 380 pages

Over 80 recipes to help you build, customize, and distribute reports using SAP BusinessObjects

1. Discover how to master different business solutions which will help you deliver high quality reports to your organization and clients.

2. Work efficiently in a BI environment while keeping your data accurate, secured, and easily shared.

3. Learn how to build and format reports that will enable you to get the most useful insights from your data.

Software Development on the SAP HANA Platform

ISBN: 978-1-84968-940-3   Paperback: 328 pages

Unlock the true potential of the SAP HANA platform

1. Learn SAP HANA from an expert.

2. Go from installation and setup to running your own processes in a matter of hours.

3. Cover all the advanced implementations of SAP HANA to help you truly become a HANA master.

Please check **www.PacktPub.com** for information on our titles